Volunteers
of the Lifeboat Service

Stephen Musgrave

Orchard Maritime Publications

Stalmine

First published 2015

Orchard Maritime Publications
Orchard Cottage,
Sarah's Fold,
Stalmine.
Poulton-le-Fylde
Lancashire

ISBN:
ISBN 978-0-9934432-0-6

DEDICATION

To my grandchildren Lewis, Katie and Jameson

to record, in part, my experience with the lifeboat service.

Especial loving thanks and appreciation to my wife Lynda for her active support, patience and assistance throughout the preparation of this book.

Front Cover: Fleetwood Lifeboat *Lady of Lancashire* on service on 25th August 1988 to assist yacht *Samsai* with 3 people on board in a Westerly gale 26 miles West of Fleetwood. Coxswain Stephen Musgrave at the helm. This photo was taken by Skipper Hughie McMillan as the lifeboat passed the Morecambe Bay Gas Field Stand-by vessel.

CONTENTS

Foreword David Pearce

Everyone in Great Britain knows something about the Lifeboat Service.

Thousands of people who live far from the coast and have little experience of the sea are happy to help the Royal National Lifeboat Institution stay afloat by donating money to this historic organisation.

They contribute because they see the R.N.L.I. rescue crews as heroes who risk their lives in the hope of saving others. Yet many of the men and women volunteers at the sharp end of the organization shun the limelight.

They seek no publicity and often play down their exploits.

However, their deeds are often both courageous and remarkable as they battle with nature in the raw out on the ocean. They might admit to sometimes enjoying the adrenalin rush of being in a fast craft on wild water. But this is no game. Life or death decisions have to be made in an instant.

The boats of the R.N.L.I. and the equipment they use have come a long way since the days of sail and oar but two things remain constant:

• The sea can be a very dangerous place both for the expert and the unwary.
• Volunteers still step forward to risk their lives crewing the lifeboats.

Stephen Musgrave speaks from experience. He was Deputy Coxswain of Fleetwood Lifeboat on the Lancashire coast and takes the reader behind the scenes for a candid look at the world of the lifeboat crew. He also examines the fundamental changes in attitude towards saving life at sea since the days when a shipwreck was seen as a miraculous bonus by coastal communities who were more concerned with pillaging the cargo than the fate of sailors.

The book is well-illustrated by pen and ink sketches from Fleetwood-based artist Ron Baxter. Like Stephen, he is a former Merchant Navy Officer.

As a boy growing up in Fleetwood with its fishing fleet, passenger ships and cargo trade of those days, I was taught to respect the men of the sea for their courage, fortitude and skill.

I believe this book will encourage others to share that respect for admirable qualities which are embodied in the work of R.N.L.I. crews.

David Pearce, journalist and local historian, Fleetwood 2015.

Foreword   John Swannie

Britain is, as she has always been, a maritime nation and those who go to sea face the perils of nature in whatever capacity they venture afloat. Shipwrecks have happened since people first ventured from the shore, and since the nineteenth century lifeboats have been stationed around the coast of the United Kingdom, crewed by volunteers and funded by public donations.

Lessons can be learned from individual misadventure, and one way is to read of the experience of those who crew the lifeboats and who have the knowledge and seamanship skills to undertake rescues in their craft. I know from personal and tragic loss of a close relative in a sea incident in Morecambe Bay that the lifeboat service is available to be called upon, at whatever time of day, and will always respond and do their utmost to rescue anyone in difficulties.

It is also true that because of the traditional enthusiasm for maritime affairs people want to read of the exploits of our life-savers and of the way they cope with the extremes of nature that they are often called out in to undertake their duties of rescue at sea. People are always inquisitive, and want to know what the coxswain and crew do to carry out individual rescues, especially in extreme circumstances and atrocious weather conditions.

The author and I were work colleagues who became friends with a shared love of sailing. We have covered many miles together over Scottish waters and in the Irish Sea. It wasn't until reading this book that I discovered the true modesty that my crewmate and dear friend disguises. I knew he'd been a lifeboat-man and indeed we have sailed in challenging conditions together but needed I to have been as concerned in these times as I was had I known of his lifeboat exploits? – probably not!

This book gave me an insight into the true bravery and determination that the R.N.L.I. crew members have, at times, to summon. It is a good read – enlightening, alarming and thoroughly enjoyable.

John Swannie

Preface

It seemed to me that far too few people who crew the lifeboats of the R.N.L.I. publish their experience of rescue incidents. Although service reports of notable incidents appear as reports in the Lifeboat journal, they fall short of giving a detailed account of the real story behind these calls. I didn't put pen to paper when I left the lifeboat service in 1990 but in recent times having discovered an ancestor who had been awarded the R.N.L.I. Silver Medal. I received an R.N.L.I. award in the 1980's and this led me to research the background of the incidents that my great-great-great-grandfather had been involved in. From that start-point investigation of rescues around Morecambe Bay, I began to research the ethics of life-saving at sea in the 1800's and so broadened the scope of this book, looking beyond Morecambe Bay and also bring the account through the 19th to the 21st centuries. I have included accounts of some of the rescues I have been involved in and some of the fool-hardy things I have done – and the lessons learned!

Having known so little of my father's life and his ancestors, a further reason for compiling this book is to record something for the sake of our children and grandchildren. I hope that perhaps in their later life they will come to read these accounts and reflect on the times I spent involved with the lifeboat service. It was a rewarding time for me and although there were a few hair-raising moments, it was a privilege to be a lifeboat crew member.

Within these pages lie some of the anecdotes and salty tales that make three decades of life-boat service such an interesting experience for me to write about. Questions abound – 'What made you join the lifeboat service as a crew member?' 'Have you ever been sea-sick?' 'What was the worst weather you went out in?' 'Have you ever had any dangerous moments?'

Volunteers of the Lifeboat Service is not intended as a history of the R.N.L.I., nor is it an autobiography. It is intended to give a perspective on the attitudes to shipwrecks and lifesaving from the nineteenth, and twentieth centuries. Knowledge and skills of seamanship were readily available in the coastal towns where lifeboats were stationed during this period. The twenty-first century has seen a need to develop the knowledge and skills of keen volunteers for the lifeboat service who may have the commitment and enthusiasm but not have a maritime background.

Accounts of a few memorable lifeboat service incidents in Fleetwood are given in detail to inform the reader of what it meant in real terms to volunteer for the lifeboat service, and still means through to this day.

The context of the book is predominantly Fleetwood oriented because in part, it is about my recollections of my time in the lifeboat service. I have purposefully widened the perspective and included a number of other incidents, mainly in the North of England to show the factors that shaped the evolution and development of the lifeboat service.

There are many people I would like to thank for their help and support in putting this book together. Particular appreciation goes to local artist Ron Baxter for his kind assistance in drawing the pen and ink sketches that have done so much to bring the pages to life.

1 INTRODUCTION

As a former lifeboat crew member I was involved with Fleetwood Lifeboat for 23 years as a crew member of Fleetwood lifeboat and served as deputy coxswain for 12 years. In the 1980's I received an R.N.L.I. service award and the R.N.L.I. Glister award with a citation for the most meritorious service and bravest act of lifesaving in a lifeboat under 10 metres (inshore lifeboat) in the UK in 1984.

This book is not about the history or technology of lifeboats. I intend to give an insight into the work of the lifeboat service and focus in particular on the people involved in individual rescues. Each chapter is discrete in its own right but there is a coherent thread that links each one as part of an overall story. I am not an historian and make no claim to great knowledge of Lifeboat history, but begin this book with an insight into events of around 150 years ago, and then more recently in the twentieth century. The content is undoubtedly historic, but I encourage you to think of the people perspective and the human lives involved in these life or death incidents. In some paragraphs the language may appear quaint but this is an inevitable consequence of sourcing information from the newspaper reportage of the mid nineteenth century.

My involvement with the lifeboat service was as a volunteer, and my early career was as a Merchant Navy Radio & Electronics Officer in the 1970's. My role involved sending messages around the globe by morse code, maintaining radar systems and electronic navigational equipment. My later career ashore took an Academic pathway, initially in Nautical Education and latterly with the Open University. I chose to train as a Radio Officer because of my interest in technology, thinking there would be a long term career in that field. Little did I know that transformative changes of satellite communications that were unheard of in the 1970's would end the need for a Radio Officer on-board ships' but I made an enjoyable career in technology ashore with the advent of the internet.

For those who may not be familiar with Fleetwood it is a former fishing port on the southern shores of Morecambe Bay, overlooking the mountains of the Lake District.

Growing up in modest circumstances in Fleetwood in the 1950's, and before we had television, a pastime was playing on the beach, including a visit to the lifeboat-house.

Fleetwood Lifeboat house and Slipway – pre 1976

Where we lived in the town was within hearing distance of the lifeboat signal maroons that were detonated to muster the lifeboat crew. I believe hearing these loud cannon-like explosive 'booms' as the lifeboat was called out on service excited interest in the lifeboat service. From a child's perspective this wooden building was almost cathedral-like. Inside the entrance the large electric winch was positioned at the top of the slipway, ready to release the lifeboat, and haul it back up again when it returned from a service call-out. We would walk past the highly polished brass propellers' and along the gloss painted sides of the lifeboat Ann Letitia Russell, as it rested high above a child's head height on its cradle at the top of the long slipway in readiness for the next service call.

Lifeboat on Slipway at Fleetwood

The great doors at the top of the slipway were normally closed, but I think the idea of going down the slipway reinforced that early interest in becoming part of the lifeboat service.

Along the walls were large sign-written boards with lists recording the rescue services carried out over the years since the nineteenth century. A model of a former 'pulling and sailing' lifeboat was on display in a glass case. The small shop selling souvenirs of ladies headscarves and Christmas cards was set up on the shelf in the window, staffed by the boathouse attendant.

Steam tug *Wyre* towing lifeboat

Near the exit door a small painting hung on the wall depicting, with Victorian exaggeration, a 19th Century scene of the life-boat being towed by the steam tug *'Wyre'* to the rescue of the sailing vessel *'Inga'*. The waves seemed mountainous and I wondered what it must be like to be a crew member of the lifeboat, little knowing at that time of the connection between this picture and my background or future interest in the lifeboat.

In 1967, at the age of eighteen, I joined the lifeboat service as a volunteer.

Fleetwood Lifeboat returning from service searching for wildfowlers near Sunderland Point, 21st October, 1973.

This picture of the *Anne Letitia Russell* lifeboat shows me (second from the left) as a crewman in October 1969. I believed at that time no-one in the family had been associated with the lifeboat service. When I was almost 40 years of age I found that I had been adopted at birth, within the family. In later life, around 2006, I met up with my birth father and he explained that his great-great grandfather William Swarbrick had been a mariner, with some connection to the lifeboat service. Through further investigations we found that my ancestor William Swarbrick in the 1860's carried out a number of rescues whilst serving as Captain of the steam tug *'Wyre'* at Fleetwood Harbour.

In the Summer of 2005 the R.N.L.I. produced a promotional booklet featuring the North West lifeboats. In Summer 2006 having met my birth father for the first time it was my wife Lynda who remembered reading an article in this brochure that mentioned the rescue that I received the R.N.L.I award for, along with the Glister award previously mentioned, and on the same page mentioned Captain William Swarbrick receiving the R.N.L.I. Silver Medal for the rescue of the crew of the barque *Pudyona* in October 1862. These were both Fleetwood rescues and it seemed a remarkable co-incidence.

Research showed that William Swarbrick had lived with his young family in Stalmine, just across the river from Fleetwood. In the 1840's it was the attraction of new employment that brought William Swarbrick and his young family from the rural farming community of Stalmine just a few miles across the River Wyre to seek employment in Fleetwood. In the mid-nineteenth century Fleetwood was a new town and with the Industrial Revolution many people were moving from elsewhere, with many changing their agricultural background to make new lives for their families in the town. Finding employment with the railway company, who operated the harbour tugs, he eventually became Captain of the Steam-tug '*Wyre*', operating from Fleetwood and the other ports of Morecambe Bay. He also qualified as a licensed Pilot, bringing ships' into and out of harbour.

2 ORIGINS OF THE LIFE-BOAT SERVICE

The lifeboat service supports a network of over 235 lifeboat stations around the coast of the United Kingdom and Ireland. Many of those stations have been in existence since the early days of the Royal National Lifeboat Institution around 150 years ago, whilst others have been established more recently in response to the need for fast inshore lifeboats in new locations. The lifeboat service in Southern Ireland retains its distinctly separate identity but is proudly part of the organisation of the lifeboat service of the UK and Ireland.

Lifeboat Silver Medal

'*Let not the deep swallow me up*' is the motto of the Royal National Lifeboat Institution. It is taken from Psalm 69 of the Holy Bible. It has been the inscription on all R.N.L.I. awards since the service was founded in Victorian times by Sir William Hillary and remains so to this day.

Before the advent of railways and the motorway network the sea-lanes around the shores of Great Britain were a natural and convenient highway, arterial for moving cargo and people around the country. In the 1800's and 1900's thousands of coastal vessels plied their trade carrying goods and raw materials to feed the needs of people and provide the raw materials to fuel the Industrial Revolution.

The unpredictable and at times relentless power of the seas has meant that shipwrecks have always happened since people first ventured afloat. Up to the end of the eighteenth century the general attitude towards shipwrecks and wreckage washed-up on the coast was morally indefensible but childishly simple. It had a logic based on a blind faith in divine Providence. A wreck was an act of God; therefore nothing must be done to prevent it because that would be interfering with God's purpose. Following a shipwreck anything left on the beach by the tide became the property of the Crown, according to the law and likely to be sold to profit the Crown. That was the Crown's own law and nobody could say it tied in with God's purpose, particularly as it was generally felt the Crown didn't need the wreckage as much as local people did in any case.

The longshoremen and the fishermen did need it; in those times they needed it desperately; so in effect a wreck and all that was in it or strewn about it belonged to anybody who could salvage it and beachcombing, still a mildly profitable side-line for some individuals in certain parts of this country, was then a full-time occupation seriously and diligently pursued.

Up to the end of the 18th century shipwrecks were seen as an opportunity for looting items washed up on the shore. By the beginning of the nineteenth century looting of wrecks by all-comers was officially frowned on and more humane attitudes prevailed. A number of organisations embarked on the task of changing the way people thought about shipwrecks. Instead of seeing them as a gift delivered by a merciful God to his suffering and deserving poor, and secretly welcoming these incidents, became considered as tragic accidents and the focus shifted from looting to salvage. In particular life-saving for those in such perilous calamities became the priority. In these times of the early nineteenth century the value of sailors' lives was disregarded and it was cargo that had to be handled carefully. This was a global issue, as reports show that when the barques Bristol and Mexico were stranded in separate incidents on the coast of Long Island, New York, America. The ship-owners, merchants, ships' captains, harbour pilots, civic leaders, and politicians appeared to be more distressed at the loss of cargo rather than they did over the lives of the dozen sailors and 203 immigrants who were lost when these vessels were wrecked.

Barque *Bristol* on 15th October, 1836.

Almost two centuries earlier, and in a completely different era as far as the ethics of saving life from shipwrecks was concerned, the barque Bristol sailed from Prince's Dock Liverpool England on 15th October, 1836, eight days before another vessel the barque Mexico.

Both vessels were carrying emigrants from England along with cargo. The Bristol arrived off the American shore on the coast of New York City on 21st November 1836 and set flag signals for a pilot to guide them through the Narrows into New York harbour. Reports show that the pilots ignored the captain's signal, preferring to keep the Sabbath. Later that evening a storm arose and strong currents drove the Bristol towards the shore. The ship grounded and pounding seas destroyed the vessels two lifeboats and waves washed over the hull trapping and drowning most of the ship's passengers.

The barque Mexico, built in 1827, sailed from Liverpool England on 23rd October 1836, eight days later than the Bristol and encountered incessant storms, taking 71 days – twice as long as the Bristol, to reach New York. Arriving on New Year's Eve the captain signalled for a pilot to take the ship into a berth in Manhattan. Another 15 vessels were also signalling for pilots, but tragically, according to local historian Arthur S. Mattson the pilots' had adjourned to a Manhattan saloon to celebrate the New Year, and while waiting for the pilots to respond to his signal, and in a rising storm, the Mexico was carried onto the Long Beach shore where it foundered. Accounts show that the ship's 111 immigrant passengers were, in the eyes of the ship's owner, merely a commodity occupying a cargo deck space leased to a passenger broker. The crew of the Mexico attempted to launch both of the ship's lifeboats but in icy water temperatures and extreme conditions both boats were lost.

Barque *Mexico* leaving Liverpool on 23rd October, 1836.

Rescue boat putting out to assist *Mexico* survivors.

A rescue boat from the shore did eventually reach the Mexico having been trailed some eight miles along the coast by a team of horses. The rescue boat took in Captain Winslow from the Mexico, 4 crew members, and 3 passengers who volunteered to crew the boat.

Wreck of *Mexico* with 108 passengers and crew abandoned to their fate

No further rescue was attempted and the remaining 108 passengers and crew were abandoned to their fate. Reports in the New York press of these two disasters were big news and newspapers readers showed they were horrified by these two events that led to the loss of 215 lives. This era was early days for investigative journalism but the wreck stories in the newspapers boosted circulation, and also captured the imagination of artists and poets. The wrecks of the Bristol and Mexico showed that in the early to mid-eighteen hundreds cargo was more valuable than immigrants lives and property, and sailors lives were of even less value, at least to businessmen and marine insurers who displayed a callous attitude to passengers. Cargo had to be handled carefully, properly stowed, and insured, unlike immigrant passengers who generally were unvalued by merchant shippers and ship captains' once they had paid their fare.

Two years later in 1838 the reportage of the Grace Darling rescue from the *Forfarshire* stranded on the Farne Islands on the North East coast of England illuminates the change in attitudes and a humane consideration for saving the lives of seafarers.

Grace Darling

Grace Darling and the Forfarshire Rescue

- This outline of the rescue from the wreck of the *Forfarshire* on the Farne Islands on the North East coast of England by Grace Darling and her father William Darling, is included to highlight the change that was happening in public attitudes to the appalling loss of life around the coast through shipwreck.

Grace Horsley Darling was born in Bamburgh on the 24th November, 1815 (the same year as the Battle of Waterloo). She was the seventh of nine children, and lived with her parents and family at the Longstone Lighthouse on the Farn Islands (or Ferne Islands as they were known locally). On the 7th September, 1838, aged 22 years, Grace and her father William Darling selflessly took their small 'coble' rowing boat to rescue nine people from the wreck of the steamer *Forfarshire* that had run aground on the notorious Harcar Rocks. This incident was sensationalised in the national press and Grace became a Victorian heroine.

Forfarshire departing River Humber on 5th September, 1838

The wooden hulled paddle steamer *Forfarshire* was built in 1834, with auxiliary rigging as a topsail schooner with a speed of 5 knots. She plied a regular route from Hull to Dundee with passengers and freight on board. Early in September 1838 she arrived in Hull having suffered boiler trouble during her southward run from Dundee. During her stay in that port a small leak was repaired in the boiler. She departed from Hull on Wednesday evening the 5th September, 1838 with 62 passengers and a cargo of freight. The weather was fair and the winds light at the time of sailing, but overnight and throughout the following day the wind increased from the NorthWest and the conditions deteriorated. It seems probable that early on Thursday a serious leak started in a boiler. A pump was used but the problem became worse and the boiler had to be shut down. Sails were set to bring the ship under control but without the steam paddles she was sluggish to handle, especially in the strong tidal current. Apparently confusing the two lighthouses on the Farne islands – the Longstone and the Inner Farne light – the captain took a course that drove the *Forfarshire* on to the rocks.

Around 4.00 a.m. early on Friday morning the 7th September, and about high-water, she struck the Harcar Rocks about a mile from the Longstone lighthouse. The ship almost immediately broke in half, and the stern section from the paddle wheel box aft sank during the night. On that fateful day William Brooks Darling, Grace's younger brother, was away fishing out of Seahouses when the ship-wreck took place and only Grace with her parents and elder sister were at the lighthouse.

During the storm Grace had been unable to sleep and around 7.00 a.m. in the early dawn she looked through her small window and saw a dark shape on Harcar Rock, and believed it was a stranded vessel. She saw movement on the rocks and realised there were survivors, and called her parents and sister. Through their telescope they were able to see a small number of people clinging to the rock.

Her father William had undertaken rescues before and knew the dangers and hazards in such conditions. He thought of waiting for a rescue boat to come from Seahouses but decided the sea may be too rough to set out from the mainland. Grace's father William decided to attempt a rescue using their 21 foot long, 4 oared, Northumbrian Coble to row to the Harcar Rock, taking Grace with him. Due to the wind direction, and knowing the tides, William decided to take a longer southerly route to gain some shelter behind the rocks and out of the worst of the stormy sea conditions.

From Sunderland Hole on the North East side of Longstone island they headed for a narrow passage called Craford's Gut, then outside Blue Caps, to land on the North side of Big Harcar, a journey of around 1 mile. As they closed on the *Forfarshire* that was lodged on the North-east tip of Harcar Rocks they could see the bow section of the vessel high on the rock, and as they approached they were able to make out more survivors than at first thought. Realising there were around 10 people William knew it would take more than one trip to get them all to the safety of the lighthouse.

William and Grace Darling in their coble.

William managed to row the Coble and manoeuvre it close enough to the rock to enable some of the survivors to get to the boat. As Grace steadied the Coble on her own William was able to reach out to a survivor and drag him to the boat. He quickly decided that he needed the strongest survivors to help row the Coble on the return trip to the Longstone Lighthouse and then row back for the second rescue attempt at the *Forfarshire* wreck. A woman was huddling her two children but they had already died so the children were placed on a high point on the rock. The mother was taken into the boat along with an injured man and two of the crew members to assist in rowing the boat.

They returned to the Longstone and having taken the survivors up to the lighthouse William and the two crewmen rowed back to the *Forfarshire* to rescue the remaining four survivors. Three bodies including the two children were left on the high point of the Harcar Rock to be recovered when the storm abated.

The whole rescue took around two hours to get the survivors back to the safety of Longstone Lighthouse.

North Sunderland Lifeboat setting out for the Farne Islands.

Meanwhile a rescue craft had set out from North Sunderland but arrived at the *Forfarshire* wreck after Grace and her father had completed the rescue. All they found were the three dead bodies of a man and two children high on the rock. They had rowed for five miles in storm force conditions, battling non-stop for two and a half hours to reach the wreckage of the *Forfarshire* at around 10.00 a.m., unaware of the major role that had been played by the Darlings. Their own strenuous effort had been fruitless.

The weather was too bad to turn around into the high seas and return to

North Shields so they decided to take refuge with the Darlings' at the Longstone lighthouse. Grace's brother William was one of the fishermen crewing the rescue craft and with great difficulty the life-boatmen reached the Longstone Lighthouse and hauled their boat up onto the rocks. Exhausted, they climbed the steps, entered the kitchen and then stood speechless. They had expected to find only Grace and her parents inside; instead there were twelve people staring back at them. William and Grace, equally shocked, thought it impossible for the North Sunderland lifeboat to launch a rescue in such conditions. A moment of shared disbelief followed, as everyone worked out what had happened - the boat had put out from North Sunderland; perhaps more remarkably, William and Grace alone, in their coble had rescued nine survivors.

The men learned with astonishment the role Grace had played in all this. William Brooks, Graces brother, was amazed at the outstanding bravery of his sister and was proud of the determination shown by his father in achieving such a rescue. After the initial acclaim however came the realisation for the seven men that having expected to eat, get warm, and find rest in the lighthouse there was actually no room for them. There were now nineteen people and only seven rooms in the lighthouse.

The seven lifeboat men had to find shelter outside as best they could in dilapidated outbuildings that flooded at every high tide. Nursing nine survivors, some sick and injured, Mrs Darling and Grace did all they could to clothe and feed their sixteen visitors but provisions were running out and the storm continued. It was three days before anyone could leave Longstone. If it had been possible to do so there is no doubt the North Sunderland men would have returned home earlier, at the first opportunity. Their families, having not heard from them, must have feared the worst.

The North Sunderland lifeboat crew would undoubtedly have reached the survivors on Harcar Rock and saved them, but the Darlings happened to get there first and they received the accolades. The brave actions of the Seahouses men went uncredited and unrewarded and their deed has been largely forgotten ever since. Quietly and without fuss they returned to their families and their ordinary lives. Life for the Darlings would never be the same again.

In 1838 although the looting of wrecks by all-comers was officially frowned on and life-saving and salvage encouraged by cash bounties, a wreck was still looked on as a gift from God Almighty to His suffering and deserving poor. The competition for the salvage bounty would have been just as keen as ever it was for the looting, and it is reasonable to suppose that the several groups of longshoremen in the vicinity – the Holy Island fishermen; the light-keepers on the Inner Farne; the North Sunderland boatmen; the Seahouses fishermen and the Darlings on the Longstone – were each informally allotted an agreed area wherein they had prior claim on whatever might be going. The rescue by William and Grace thus became an issue with the Seahouses fishermen who had put out in their rescue boat to the Harcar, only to discover that the lighthouse keeper had been 'on their patch'.

However, the Victorian press picked up on this story of rescue. Who first referred to the *Forfarshire* rescue as Grace Darling's 'deed' is not known now; but the term has stuck and recurs in each successive biography suitably embellished with adjectives like 'brave', 'courageous', 'fearless', 'valiant', 'noble', 'indomitable', 'intrepid', 'daring', and 'selfless' according to the fancy and fundamental values of the author.

Biographers and journalists portrayed Grace as a heroine – the girl with the wind blown hair – but this was only part of the story, and it was to lead to a tragic and untimely end for Grace who was uncomfortable with the celebrity status and who died at the age of just 26 as a result of consumption.

Another fact in the overall story was that the *Forfarshire* was a steamboat in the age of sail. She was built in 1834. Before that, generations of men, both practical engineers and dreamers, had been fascinated by the promise of steam. Here, if only it could be harnessed, was the power that would give a man the strength of giants and make him master of all nature and independent of its moods. It was the steam itself, the new source of infinite power, seemingly limitless in its application and cheap beyond belief, that was the lure. On shore textile mills, metal foundries and all the pioneering developments of the Industrial Revolution were turning over from small-scale operation by hand or water power to steam.

As yet only a handful of shipbuilders and ship-owners were adopting steam power; for if this was the beginning of the age of steam navigation, it was also the heyday of the sailing ship, which was making great strides forward and attaining new heights of achievement in size and speed. Sailing ships owed nothing to the Industrial Revolution, and the men who designed and made them wanted nothing to do with steam navigation. They built their ships' of the finest hardwoods in the world, English oak and Malabar teak. Those who had committed themselves and their future to steam went on building their smoke belching vessels, making them larger and larger and shouting louder and louder about them.

Against this background of tensions over *Rescue on my patch'* by the North

Sunderland fishermen; sail versus steam; and the overall desire to promote the humanitarian cause of saving people from shipwreck, such institutions as the humane societies, that were the nascent lifeboat organisations and the groups agitating for legislation to make travel by sea less hazardous played it up for all it was worth to boost their humanitarian cause.

Fifteen years earlier than the rescue from the *Forfarshire* Sir William Hillary in the town of Douglas, Isle of Man, published in 1823 a pamphlet entitled An Appeal to the British Nation on the Humanity and Policy of forming a National Institution for the Preservation of Lives and Property from Shipwreck. At a meeting in London the following year in 1824 the National Institution for the Preservation of Life from Shipwreck was formed.

Unfortunately the organisation became popularly known as the Shipwreck Institution, and in 1854 its name was changed to Royal National Lifeboat Institution. Over the 160 years since the founding of the R.N.L.I. and 190 years since Hillary held the meeting in London the R.N.L.I. has stayed true to the blueprint that Hillary, with extraordinary prescience offered in his 1823 pamphlet.

Napoli off Branscombe Beach 22nd January, 2007.

Taking items from wrecks was evident on 22nd January 2007 when the Container ship *Napoli* grounded off Branscombe in South Devon, near Weymouth, and over 50 expensive BMW motorcycles were being taken from the containers washed up along the shore.

The following year on 31st January 2008 the roll-on roll-off container vessel *Riverdance* was stranded on the beach off Blackpool. All the crew were successfully taken off by helicopter and Fleetwood Lifeboat gave assistance, but all that washed ashore from a container were digestive biscuits!

Fleetwood Lifeboat standing by the Ro-Ro vessel Riverdance on 31st January, 2008.

Fleetwood Life-boat gave assistance and stood-by the vessel throughout the night of this incident supporting an R.A.F. rescue helicopter as they lifted off all the crew to safety. For newly appointed coxswain Paul Ashworth this was his first call as coxswain and must have been a difficult night.

Through the accounts in this chapter the reader can see the decades of the early eighteen hundreds were a transformational period in the attitudes of people towards shipwrecks and life-saving at sea. Humane concern prevailed towards seafarers in distress and organisations and governments around the world have established bodies responsible for rescue of those in peril on the seas. The ethics and humanity that led to the formation of the R.N.L.I. with its motto *'Let not the Deep Swallow me up'* are still as relevant and valid in the 21st century as they have been over the past two centuries. The lifeboat service continues to rely on volunteers, and it is still a voluntarily funded organisation.. Naturally many improvements have been made in lifeboat design and construction, yet the single most important factor is the crew members, for without their skill and bravery the best materials would be useless. Changes in technology continue to impact on lifesaving at sea, along with the changes in human attributes described in the next chapter to match the needs of a 21st century Lifeboat service.

3 THE VOLUNTEERS

The volunteers of the life-boat service provide a dependable service around the entire coastline of the United Kingdom and Ireland, 24 hours a day, 365 days each year. With an average number of 25 calls every day on the lifeboat service in weather conditions ranging from the benign to the extreme of violent storms. Although many calls on the life-boat crews' may appear mundane, every service is uniquely special to the individuals who have summoned the assistance of a lifeboat in their hour of need. Lifeboat crews' are ever mindful of this in the way they conduct themselves. On occasions the life-boats are called upon in extreme weather conditions where a coxswain and the crew are called upon to apply their skill and knowledge in literally saving lives that otherwise may have been lost. For those people who find themselves in a distress situation at sea the moment the life-boat arrives alongside them cannot be underestimated as they realise that rescue is at hand.

A Volunteer for the Lifeboat. Artist Mrs M.D. Webb Robinson   Lowry Collection

This famous painting from the same era titled 'A Volunteer for the Lifeboat' that hangs in the Lowry Collection in Salford, Manchester gives a sense of the emotions surrounding the act of volunteering to crew the rowing lifeboat on a stormy day.

Southport Lifeboat survivor John Jackson.

This image of John Jackson, a survivor from the Southport lifeboat crew involved in the attempted rescue from the barque Mexico, and depicted in his oilskin suit, cork life-vest, and sou'wester hat, appears to be the epitome of a life-boatman in the nineteenth century. Throughout the nineteenth and into the early part of the twentieth century the main attributes required of crew members were physical strength and the ability to pull on an oar for extended periods, along with seamanship knowledge and skills. Anecdotally it was this image that was used for the monument that commemorates this tragedy in St. Annes. The lifeboat service continues to this day to be a voluntary organisation, funded entirely by public subscription (as explained in Chapter 4 – Fundraising) and operated by volunteer crew-members. In the 21st century, as it was in the 20th century, this seems to be an anachronism and people often ask the question why should such an essential life-saving operation continue to rely on volunteers? This issue is addressed towards the end of this chapter.

In any rescue incident there are typically three discrete phases: transporting crew from the lifeboat station to the scene of the incident; doing the tricky business that may be required to rescue those in difficulty; and returning back to the lifeboat station, hopefully with survivors. Each rescue is individual and at the outset the information may be sparse and it may be necessary to conduct a search to find those in distress. The personal attributes of lifeboat crew include the need for strength in the face of adversity, and in particular perseverance and vigilance, especially on long searches that may be in bad weather and darkness. Physical stamina and mental alertness of everyone on board the life-boat is needed to ensure concentration on the task in hand, especially when a search goes on over a prolonged period and perhaps over a wide sea area. It is not always possible to save lives but when individuals lose their lives you need to have that peace of mind that at least you tried your utmost as a team to do your best with the scenario presented to you.

A lifeboat may seem to be an inanimate object resting on a cradle at the top of a slipway, or lying afloat on a mooring on in a lifeboat dock but when she goes to sea the lifeboat becomes a vibrant and purposeful living entity, pulsing with the power thrust of its machinery and the energy of the crew. When the maroons go to announce a service call there is undoubtedly an initial adrenalin rush for each crew member but once at sea and with information about the nature of the casualty in distress the lifeboat becomes alive. Proceeding at full speed in an offshore lifeboat and surrounded at the steering position with position fixing electronic charts, radar display and communication systems, information is available to the coxswain and his team coordinate the search and rescue, taking decision, assigning tasks, thinking ahead in anticipating risks and constantly reviewing the scenario as new information is available. The lifeboat has a 'buzz' about it as every crew member is concentrating on their own role cocooned in the cabin as they head towards the casualty, often in heavy seas as the lifeboat rides the waves at full service speed. The same experience exists in an inshore lifeboat, with its crew but being exposed to the elements and leaping from wave-crest to wave-crest the crew are also getting a soaking in their immersion suits.

Consideration of the changes in people attributes for a 21st century lifeboat service requires a reflection on the 'people' attributes of earlier lifeboat

characters. Pictured here is Coxswain Richard Evans from Moelfre in North Wales. He was in the lifeboat service for 50 years and was awarded the Gold Medal in 1959 and again in 1966. I met Dick when we used to take the Fleetwood Lifeboat to a boatyard in North Wales, and he was a well known personality across the country. He was considered to be a lifeboatman's lifeboatman, stereotypical of his era. (said to be The Queen Mother's favourite life-boatman when she was alive).

Coxswain 'Dick' Evans

He had originally planned a life at sea, becoming a cabin boy on a coaster at the age of 14, progressing to master mariner at the age of 23. But his family recalled him to work in their butchers shop in Moelfre. In 1954 he became coxswain of the lifeboat. Five years on he won the Gold medal for his rescue of the crew of the coaster *Hindlea*. In 1966, at the age of 61, he won his second Gold medal for his role in rescuing the crew of the Greek freighter *Nafsiporus* on 2nd December 1966. The Holyhead lifeboat was also involved in this incident and a later lifeboat friend Eric Jones, who worked in the Trinity House depot in Holyhead was awarded the Silver medal in the same incident, whilst a crewman on the Holyhead life-boat. Richard Evans died in 2001 at the age of 96 and a statue has been erected near the Moelfre Lifeboat station in tribute to his service with the R.N.L.I..

Dick Wright

A photograph of Fleetwood Lifeboat station personnel in 1933 shows third from the left Richard Wright, who became coxswain of Fleetwood Lifeboat.

Both Dick Evans and Dick Wright were tough no-nonsense characters who were decisive and single-minded. Knowledgeable and experienced seamen they seemed to epitomise the lifeboatman of the era I grew up in.

Importantly they had a working knowledge of their geographic area. They were fishing their 'patch' daily and had an intimate awareness of the hazards, currents, tides and obstructions. Coxswain Dick 'Cush' Wright was an inshore fisherman, owning his Morecambe Bay Prawner named *Judy*. More often than not the men who sailed them owned them and these inshore fishing boats were named after a family member, but in this case Dick had bought his boat second hand following the loss of his previous vessel.

In the fishing community because there were often many members of the same family with the surnames such as Wright or Leadbetter, and often more than one person with the same Christian name and surname, so nicknames were assigned to individuals. Many nicknames had biblical links and Dick's nickname was *Cush*. (In the Bible Cush was the grandson of Noah, father of Nimrod The Hunter and there is mention of a Land of Cush thought to be around Egypt, Saudi Arabia and Ethiopia– why the nickname *Cush* was given to him is uncertain). As a young lad of around 12 years old I - like many young lads - used to go on 12 hour 'pleasure trips' on boats of the inshore fishing fleet in the Summer. There wasn't much pleasure if the wind freshened and my role was limited to 'stand there' in the cockpit, and don't go out on deck. I distinctly remember the tins of condensed milk that were used in making mugs of tea, the sickly smell and the nauseating effect it could have on you if you were already feeling slightly unwell with sea-sickness but it was a formative life experience that left a deep impression on my character and fond memories of a formative life experience.

Morecambe Bay Prawner *Judy*

Dick Wright's father had been coxswain and Dick himself had been awarded an illuminated vellum from the R.N.L.I. for the part he played in the rescue of the crew from the Faroese fishing schooner *Stella Marie* in 1941. Although he had been a fisherman and involved with the lifeboat service for most of his adult life he had never learned how to swim. The story of this rescue is told in Chapter 6. In his later life he told a story of being called out as a crew member on the lifeboat on Christmas Day 1929 to rescue the 7 crew from the *S.S.Tchad* of Le Havre, a former passenger steamer anchored near Lune Deeps awaiting being taken for scrapping. The *S.S. Tchad* sent up distress signals as its anchor was dragging in extremely bad weather. *'Cush'* recalled that the wind was so strong that the tapes tying his sou-wester helmet were torn away and with no spares hats on-board for the remainder of the service he had no head protection against the salt spray that was continually being driven by the strong winds. Since that day he had remained deaf in the ear that had been exposed to this weather.

As a lifeboat crewman in many ways I feel that I was in the right place at the right time in life-boating terms in that the replacement of the Ann Letitia Russell lifeboat was a significant step change, with the introduction of new technology into the lifeboat fleet. Not only was the speed twice as fast, but the boat had radar, vhf radio direction finders and other sophisticated equipment that suited my background interest. For the first time we reliably knew where we were in any conditions, which was a considerable development. I considered myself to be a thinking life-boatman, able to use the new equipment resources to good effect. With the radar we could undertake expanding box searches in a way not previously possible. Nowadays, with electronic charts and satellite navigation it is possible to programme in courses to individual locations accurately.

From the early days of the inception of the lifeboat service women volunteers have played an important role not only in fund-raising for the R.N.L.I. charity, but also in launching the lifeboat, and as lifeboat crew members. Since the latter part of the 20th Century the numbers of female crew members on the lifeboats have increased and nowadays women form part of the lifeboat crew at most stations around the UK.

When on New Year's Day, 1861. The ship 'Lovely Nellie' had been wrecked off Whitley Bay the storm prevented the lifeboat being launched at Cullercoats. It had to be towed by horses and villagers three miles along coast.

'The Women' by John Charlton, The Laing Gallery.

This painting depicts the lifeboat coming over the hill and down the steep slope of Briar Dene to launch in the next Bay. Women of the community as Fish Wives were supporting their menfolk in turning out to help with the lifeboat, knowing that it could be their partners one day that needed assistance.

Launch of Runswick Bay Lifeboat by the Women. Artist T. Brown
Courtesy of Kirkleatham Museum Redcar

A similar scene is depicted in this painting set in Runswick Bay, between Whitby and Staithes on the Yorkshire Coast. A first impression is that of a sexist portrayal of a scene with the men keeping their feet dry while the women wade into the water to pull on ropes to launch the lifeboat. However, a study of records for the event portrayed here reveals a different scenario. After a severe and harsh winter and when most of the fishermen of Runswick, who happened to be the lifeboat crew, were trying to get some income and were caught out in an unexpected storm in April 1901. They hadn't expected bad weather and after the long winter had started their fishing season early to get some money, setting out in fair weather they had all simply been caught out by an unexpected change. Their wives and children were left ashore knowing that each of their menfolk were in danger and signalling their distress. It was the wives and partners of those fishermen out at sea who launched the lifeboat while a scratch crew of mainly elderly and retired life-boatmen were found to go to the rescue.

Women launching the lifeboat

In this post First World-war photograph women had launched the lifeboat during the war when men of the village were away in the armed forces: the lifeboat crew members being replaced by retired crew members who may be in their 70's and women pulling the ropes to launch the lifeboat.

As a volunteer crew member, people sometimes ask you what was the worst weather you have experienced on a lifeboat. In my case I vividly recall an incident on Sunday afternoon 27th October, 1974. The maroons had been fired and in strong wind conditions we drove down to the life-boathouse. It was around an hour before low-tide and the slipway length was about 200 feet to the water's edge of the river. I was a young crewman aged 25 years. With the crew dressed in oilskins and lifejackets and on-board the lifeboat, the engines started and all preparations to launch the boat completed the signal was given to 'knock out' the release shackle that held the lifeboat in position at the top of the slipway. As soon as the boat emerged from the shelter of the lifeboat-house itself and trundled down the slipway we experienced the full force of the wind and it was 'howling' – Northwesterly Storm Force 10.

Service Boards, Fleetwood

Quite incredibly and never experienced before in over 100 years at Fleetwood Lifeboat station, before the boat reached the water it slowed due to the pressure of the wind blowing sideways across the slipway pinning the lifeboat against the slipway runner and stopping the boat short of the water.

Fleetwood Lifeboat stopped on slipway

This was a major problem because whilst it takes under 10 seconds for the boat to roll down the slipway to the bottom it takes around 20 minutes to winch the boat back up again in preparation to re-launch; and this is what had to be done. As the boat was slowly winched back up the slip the rollers and slipway were given extra grease to smooth the next launch. After this delay the lifeboat was launched again and although the boat got slightly further down the slipway the storm-force wind pressing on the side of the boat stopped the lifeboat for a second time. The weather at this time was extreme with squally rain showers and no decrease in the wind strength that was gusting at Hurricane force 11. A large crowd had gathered to witness this event and once again it was necessary to winch the boat back up the slipway again. Wind-blown sand was exacerbating the problem in settling on the slipway and acting as an abrasive brake. As the boat was hauled up the slipway the grease was scraped away from the slipway keel channel (as blown sand had mixed with the grease forming an abrasive compound) in preparation for another attempt and the Fire Brigade attended to use their powerful hosepipes to wash any sand down the slipway into the river.

Third successful launch of the lifeboat

Just before launching the slipway was greased again and on the third attempt - although slowing down with the pressure of wind - the boat entered the water to the cheers of the assembled crowd.

Having launched the boat some 2 hours after the initial call we then realised that our problems were just beginning, because the weather was simply atrocious and we started to speculate on what we could do under such conditions.

Proceeding up channel in bad weather

The sea was very rough in the river and the wind was still severe gale force 9, with stronger gusts as we proceeded along the 2 mile channel into the open seas of Morecambe Bay. The Coaster *Rolf* was the casualty and she was a German coastal cargo vessel registered in Hamburg, with seven crew members on board. They had left Glasson Dock – the Lancaster port on the previous tide but experienced heavy weather and turned back and anchored in the Bay, but with deteriorating conditions the crew were finding that the anchor was not holding the seabed, even though they were still using the engines and they were slowly dragging towards the shore.

Tug proceeding from Heysham

In the appalling weather conditions it was decided that as they were not in immediate danger and did not want to abandon their vessel, and because a large tug from Heysham was preparing to come out to assist, the lifeboat would standby the *Rolf* and only attempt to take off the crew if the vessel dragged closer to the shore and started pounding on the sandbanks.

The tug was expected within the hour and it became a matter of looking after ourselves, and dodging the seas whilst waiting for the tug to arrive. I learned a big lesson in this time - that as long as you are not trying to proceed at speed into these seas it is a case that even in the roughest seas you can point the boat slightly off the wind and 'bob' about like a cork quite comfortably, and as long as there is enough water beneath you are quite safe and in control of the situation.

'the seas were simply tremendous'

It was dark by this time and the seas were simply tremendous, and unlike anything I had previously encountered in my life, but there was both an awesomeness and a serenity in the situation. Standing outside on the open deck as each sea approached the lifeboat slowly rose up the face of the wave until sitting on the crest and equally slowly descending down the back as the wave rolled past. The Rolf was continuing to drift slowly down towards the sandbanks even with its engines engaged and its anchor down, and during this period the coxswain Roy Mitchinson considered the options. The problem would be that there was insufficient water at the site where the Rolf was anchored for the tug to get close enough.

'an awesomeness and a serenity in the situation'

On the Radio-telephone the situation was discussed between the tug Captain, the Captain of the 'Rolf', and the life-boat coxswain and a plan was formulated. The proposal was to use the lifeboat as an intermediary, enabling the tug to remain in deep water and pass a towing cable to the Rolf - using the lifeboat.

As the coxswain manoeuvred the lifeboat alongside the tug a crew member prepared to fire a rocket line from the lifeboat to the after deck of the tug. This is literally a hit or miss operation because contrary to expectations the rocket doesn't travel in a straight line; it seeks up into the wind, and the light line attached to the rocket drifts down wind. We had practiced this drill on exercises but never fired a line-throwing rocket in such extreme conditions. The drill includes estimating how far upwind to point the line thrower to aim the rocket so that the trailing line will fall where intended.

The wind and sea conditions were simply outside our experience, and on the pitching deck of the lifeboat it was difficult to prop oneself in a way that you could reliably fire the rocket. The rocket-line container trigger was squeezed and after a moments delay the rocket hurtled through the air with its trailing line.

The risk was not only in the direction of the rocket's trajectory but if it was too low the line would drop into the sea before reaching the tug, and too

Firing rocket line across to the tug

high and the line could overshoot and drop behind the tug; not to mention the possibility of the rocket striking the hull of the tug. However, it was a bulls-eye shot and the line dropped on the afterdeck of the tug and was secured by the tug crew members.

The rocket-line was attached to a towrope from the tug, which in turn was secured to the heavy wire hawser that was to be passed to the Rolf. The weather remained extreme and the Rolf was continuing its slow drift towards shallow water and the treacherous sandbanks. Slowly the lifeboat was manoeuvred stern first with the rope and hawser attached to the front of the lifeboat as the lifeboat coxswain manoeuvred across the gap between the tug in deep water and the Rolf in the breaking waves close inshore. Another crew member had the second rocket-line prepared and when we were close alongside the Rolf a rocket-line was fired across. This line missed but another rocket was prepared and this carried a line across and was attached at this second attempt. The hawser was eventually attached to the Rolf and the tug commenced the tow towards Heysham. The lifeboat escorted the tug and Rolf to Heysham, and returned to station at 23.30 hours, after nine and a half hours on service.

As the weather abated by the next day the Rolf sailed from Heysham twenty four hours later, resuming its passage to Germany with no damage sustained and all the crew safe.

Towrope from tug on lifeboat's bow, and firing second rocket line across to the *Rolf*

Although this attempted rescue was carried out in extreme weather conditions the lifeboat service boards simply record 'Stood by vessel' – a factually accurate yet masterly understatement of the role played by the lifeboat in this incident.

Concluding this chapter on the volunteers of the lifeboat service - regardless of the lifeboat being self-righting or non self-righting, steel, wooden, or fibre composite construction; filled with sophisticated instrumentation, or a humble inflatable Inshore Life Boat, the traditions of the lifeboat service continue. The crews of today are still volunteers aided by electronic charts, radar, radio direction finders, echo-sounders and all the refinements of modern technology, but the sea is still as challenging and will always have its moods. Lifeboat crews need their courage, knowledge and seafaring skills as never before when tackling rescues far out to sea and at a range of 100 miles from shore that not so long ago would have been deemed impossible. Through the innovation of lifeboat design, engine reliability and use of advanced technology any loss of life is minimised and lifeboat disasters are rare. Of course circumstances have sometimes become so overwhelming that the lifeboats and their crew have been lost. Such was the case in Fraserburgh in the North East of Scotland; Longhope in the Orkneys; and Penlee in Cornwall.

The lifeboat service continues to operate in its voluntary tradition and is predicted to remain that way into the long term future. So in partial answer to the question - why do lifeboat crews volunteer for the lifeboat? In the

1800's the payment of a gold sovereign (£1), was a helpful payment but it had to be more than this to get someone to risk their life. Surely, it can't be for the sheer love of it? The answer is probably linked to a motive of altruism – unselflessness as a principle of action. In the 1800's when the coastline was so important for both moving goods as cargo, and for fishing communities, there must have been a strong element of 'It could be me out there'. To do nothing when people could be seen to be in distress was not an option.' This also picks up on of the founding principles from William Hillary's original paper that rescue would be regardless of nationality, that to this day follows this humane principle of helping anyone in difficulty at sea.

An advantage of the use of volunteers in lifeboat crews' is that they are essentially local people and as such have knowledge and experience of their geographic operating area.

As a strategic development the R.N.L.I. now recruits individuals who may have the enthusiasm and commitment to become a lifeboat crew member but may need to be taught new skills and gain new knowledge in seamanship. A bespoke training programme at the recently opened Lifeboat College at the R.N.L.I headquarters in Poole, Dorset, enables individuals to become competent as a life-boat person.

In the nineteenth and early 20th century the fishing community was thriving around the coast of the UK and fishermen with their skills and knowledge were the main source of crew for the lifeboat. In the latter half of the 20th century the numbers of volunteer crew members who earned their living at sea, either in the fishing community, the Merchant Navy or on commercial coastal craft was diminishing. In the 21st century there aren't the same numbers of people who have sea skills and whether the lifeboat crew members are men or women an increasing problem for the lifeboat service was a skills deficit. The lifeboat service has confronted this issue and factored into its development a strategy to 'grow its own' knowledge and skills base, by introducing training programmes and a framework for skills development for its crew. At the Lifeboat College headquarters in Poole crew are trained from a basic induction programme through to advanced skills in the sophisticated systems on board the lifeboats. Also, up to the latter days of the twentieth century with an offshore lifeboat typically having up to eight crew a lifeboat station may have around fifteen crew members it could call upon, and each of these would live and mainly work in reasonable proximity of the lifeboat station. Nowadays employers may be less willing to allow their staff to drop what they are doing at work and go out on a lifeboat call, and so most lifeboat stations recruit and train many more personnel than they need and operate some form of shift system whereby volunteers are available on certain days, or weeks, within each month.

Stephen Musgrave

4 Fund-raising

The R.N.L.I. relies on voluntary contributions and this chapter on fund-raising begins with an outline account of the worst tragedy of the lifeboat service that happened in the late 19th century. It was the St Annes and Southport lifeboat disaster that led one businessman, Mr Charles Macara (later Sir Charles Macara) and his wife, to fundamentally change the way that funds were raised, not only to provide the life-boats themselves but also to reward the crew for service calls. Since the early formation of Shipwreck Societies and the inception of the Royal National Lifeboat Institution the idea of reward and recognition has been present, and is still exists today.

The tragic incident at St Annes and Southport on the night of 9th December, 1886, causes that year to stand out in the history of the Royal National Lifeboat Institution, just as 1066 stands out in the history of England – though the R.N.L.I. incident is not so universally known.

In this incident three lifeboat towns of Lytham, Southport, and St. Annes in Lancashire responded to the distress of a vessel and two of the lifeboats failed to return.

The barque 'Mexico' was an iron-hulled vessel built at Sunderland in 1860, and originally named John Bull. Her name was changed to Mexico when she was purchased by a Hamburg ship-owner. (She was a different vessel to the one of the same name 'Mexico' in Chapter 2) On the 5th of December, 1886 the 'Mexico' sailed from Liverpool bound for Guayaquil in Ecuador, on the West coast of South America, fully laden with a general cargo. This voyage would have necessitated the rounding of Cape Horn in the South Atlantic.

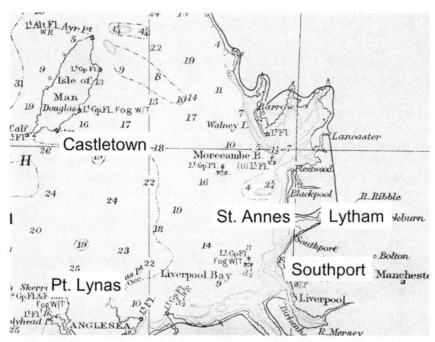

Chart of area showing Liverpool, Lytham, St. Annes and Southport Source: Admiralty

The geography of the area in the North Irish Sea and Liverpool Bay is shown in this Admiralty Chart section outlining the North West coastline of England; the Isle of Man; the North Wales coastline; and Anglesey.

Lytham is nowadays a wealthy town, described as 'Leafy Lytham' and with one of the highest number of millionaires per capita in the country.   In the Victorian era of the 1860's Lytham was a small fishing village with considerable poverty. St. Annes just a couple of miles westward along the estuary of the River Ribble was the prosperous neighbour as a genteel seaside resort of St. Annes on Sea. It also had two sides to it, again with poverty in the fishing community. Southport like St. Annes had similarly contrasting prospects, a residential town within easy commuting distance of Liverpool with large residential houses and an impoverished fishing community. The life of seafarers on this coast was a precarious one, with their income largely dependent upon the chance of good weather to go fishing. Due to silting problems and shortage of water on the foreshore the fishing boats were unable to operate and its fisher-folk were moving their families to the new port of Fleetwood, twenty miles north.

Barque 'Mexico' departing Liverpool 5th December, 1886

On the morning of Sunday 5th December 1886 the gales of the previous two days had moderated and at 10.00 a.m. the Mexico slipped her lines in the Liverpool Dock and moved out into the River Mersey.

The wind was from the South-west and she made only slow progress. During the day the wind moderated and veered round into the NorthWest. The visibility was very good, but there was still a sea running from the previous bad weather.

The Mexico was under full sail but it took until noon on Tuesday the 7th of December, before she dropped the pilot at Point Lynas on the North-East tip of Anglesey, a distance of only around 70 miles. Around 10.00 p.m. on the same day they sighted Langness Point, near Castletown on the South-East corner of the Isle of Man. The lighthouse on Douglas Head further along the East coast was also visible. The weather was deteriorating and around midnight the wind had increased to gale force, with heavy rain and hail showers. As the night went on the wind continued to strengthen, and the seas became mountainous.

By Wednesday afternoon the westerly wind had reached storm force. The Mexico was being carried off course towards the North Wales coast, and around 3.00 a.m. on the 9th of December the lighthouse at Great Orme Head, near Llandudno was sighted about twelve miles away.

Four days after departing the Liverpool port the barque *'Mexico'* was still unable to get beyond Liverpool Bay. Altering to a northerly course to gain distance from the coast of Wales, and around 1.00 p.m. on the 9th of December land was sighted to leeward on the starboard bow, and this was believed to be Formby Point, near Southport. With the wind still blowing hard from the North West the *'Mexico'* was being forced onto a lee shore.

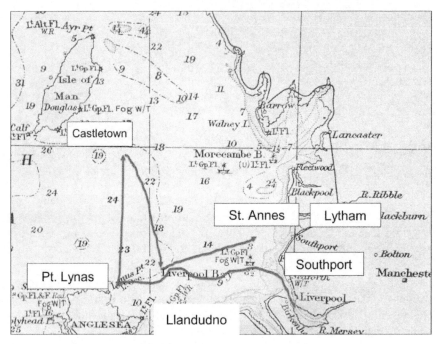

Chart showing track of the 'Mexico' after four days   Source: Admiralty

Captain Burmester of the 'Mexico'

As the afternoon went on Captain Burmester of the *'Mexico'*, realised that in the continuing conditions any hope of sailing away from this shore was rapidly vanishing. Some of his crew had sailed with him for over 25 years, and now they were recognising the difficulty and danger of their perilous situation. Depth sounding showed around 15 fathoms (90 feet) of water. An anchor was dropped to try to hold the sea-bed and stop the drift towards the shore. Work was started on cutting down the masts to reduce the windage and slow the drift towards the shore. The ropes supporting the masts were chopped and in a couple of minutes, aided by the violent movement of the ship, the foremast fell over the starboard side, smashing the ship's boat on the main-deck and damaging the deck-house and the starboard bulwark. It took half an hour to get the foremast rigging clear of the bowsprit, and with the anchor failing to hold the sea-bed the ship was dragging towards the shore. The depth soundings had reduced to 12 fathoms (around 70 feet). A similar operation was undertaken with the main-mast and it was after dark, and in atrocious conditions, before this operation was completed. In this operation Captain Burmester fell, breaking 2 ribs.

A second anchor was dropped, with 60 fathoms of warp, to attempt to stop the Mexico dragging. The anchor gripped the sea-bed but with tremendous seas running the port cable soon parted at the anchor winch, and shortly afterwards the starboard cable snapped, leaving the Mexico drifting down onto a lee shore. A further desperate attempt was made in dropping a small anchor, with a five inch hemp rope, but that also broke. More than six hours after the operation to cut down the masts commenced, and between

8.00 p.m. and 9.00 p.m. on the 9th of December the dismasted hull of the Mexico with the remnant debris of its for'ard and main mast and rigging over the side slowly drifted past four black buoys close on the starboard side.

'Mexico' hull with just mizzen mast remaining

Soon afterwards the hull struck the seabed with a resounding shudder, and seas started to break over the vessel. To indicate their plight the crew made a distress flare with an iron bar wrapped with oakum caulking dipped in turpentine spirit. This light was burned and replenished about every twenty minutes until around midnight.

Lytham lifeboat 'Charles Biggs' launching

The distress signal was seen from the shore at Lytham at around 09.30 p.m., on a bearing South West from the boathouse, and the Lytham lifeboat *'Charles Biggs'* was successfully launched at five minutes past ten. The tide was approaching high water when she set off down the River Ribble under oars for a distance of about a mile and a half. The sails were then hoisted and a course South-South-West steered, taking the lifeboat over the Horse Bank in the direction of the wreck. In the distance they could make out a small light that eventually turned out to be a lantern hoisted on the remaining Mizzen mast of the Mexico. The wind was from West-North-West and the seas were on the starboard beam, filling the boat four or five times as they headed towards the light that they could now see along with the outline shape of a ship's hull. When the lifeboat was about a quarter of a mile from the ship the sails were lowered and stowed in preparation to row the final distance to get alongside the vessel. As this was taking place a heavy breaking sea struck the lifeboat, tipping her over to port until her side was under water, and breaking three oars. The lifeboat rolled back and recovered without further damage or loss and the coxswain was able to continue under oar to the stricken vessel, successfully getting alongside the *'Mexico'*.

The *'Mexico'* crew had reported seeing a green light answering signal burning on shore, and later saw another green signal. Suddenly in the blackness of the night and with heavy seas pounding the vessel on the sandbank the Mexico's crew saw a boat on their starboard side, two points before the beam. About ten to fifteen minutes later, at between 12.30 a.m.

and 1.00 a.m., the Lytham lifeboat was alongside the Mexico and could hear the shouts from the crew who were lashed to the mast stumps and rigging. The lifeboat anchor was dropped and the lifeboat veered down on the casualty.

Lytham lifeboat approaching stern of stranded 'Mexico'

Great difficulty was experienced in getting to the survivors as waves were constantly breaking over the Mexico, and hail and sleet showers continued unabated. The first rope that was thrown to the crew of the Mexico was attached but broke as a wave pushed the lifeboat away. Another rope was thrown and the crew started to clamber across to the lifeboat. Two of the 'Mexico's crew were injured in the transfer, but with all eleven crew and the Mexico's captain on board the Lytham lifeboat the anchor was retrieved, the rope released, enabling the lifeboat to move away from the 'Mexico', but another oar was broken as a wave caught the lifeboat. By this time the tide was ebbing and in the process of putting the mast back up and setting the sail the lifeboat twice bumped on the sandy bottom of the river.

Lytham lifeboat 'Charles Biggs' returning to station with crew of 'Mexico' on board.

The lifeboat coxswain asked Captain Burmester of the *Mexico* where they would like to be landed. He replied "You have a fine boat. Where you go I go". With the sail hoisted and clear of the sea-bed the lifeboat slowly clawed its way into deeper water and headed back towards Lytham. As the lifeboat was clear of the stranded vessel a green hand-flare was lit to

Lytham lifeboat 'Charles Biggs' arriving back at Lytham.

indicate to the shore that the crew had been rescued. The lifeboat arrived at Lytham Pool under oars at around 3.30 a.m. with the survivors from the Mexico, to the great rejoicing of the crowd on the shore. The rescued and the rescuers were soaked to the skin and generally half-drowned with salt encrusted in their beards and in every line of their faces.

At this time they were unaware of the disaster that had befallen the other crews from St. Annes and Southport.

Southport lifeboat 'Eliza Fernley' launching

On the shore in Southport the signals of distress had been seen at around 9.00 p.m. The team of horses was harnessed to the lifeboat trailer and with the crew assembled the boat was towed some three and a half miles along the shore. This was a favourable position to launch the lifeboat to the westward of the stricken vessel so that it could be rowed down the following seas to the casualty. The Southport Lifeboat had sixteen crew members instead of the usual 13. Three men who were entitled to go on the boat and had arrived first at the lifeboat station had gone to fetch horses, and while they were away thirteen others put on lifejackets. The coxswain told the crew that so many could not go but they all insisted – and a *little bit of bother* ensued. Before deciding who he should take, the coxswain asked the Honorary Secretary what should be done and he advised the coxswain to take them all as he would need them and to double bank the oars. Further, if he did not, the men would object and the launch would be delayed. It was reported that so many men had actually turned up to volunteer that there were enough to man another boat.

The Southport lifeboat *'Eliza Fernley'* reached the Mexico at approximately 1.00 a.m. The coxswain positioned the lifeboat ahead of the Mexico on her starboard bow to set the lifeboat's anchor and veer down on the wreck but as the crew were about to release the anchor a heavy breaking sea struck the lifeboat and capsized her. The lifeboat never self-righted, perhaps because it was encumbered by the anchor and its rope.

'Eliza Fernley' lifeboat capsized near *'Mexico'*

When the *'Eliza Fernley'* life-boat capsized several of the crew were trapped under the boat entangled in lines and gear but John Jackson and three others found themselves clinging to the outside of the hull. As the upturned hull was driven shoreward the men clinging to the hull received a terrible beating from the waves, their strength soon started to leave them in the bitter conditions and three of them were carried away into the darkness leaving only John Jackson.

Another man, Henry Robinson, had been trapped underneath the upturned hull. Eventually the wreck of the Eliza Fernley struck the bottom and Henry Robinson felt sand under has feet and could hear the roar of the surf breaking on the beach.

'Eliza Fernley' lifeboat capsized near *'Mexico'*

He managed to crawl out from beneath the hull of the capsized boat and make for the shore. The waves tumbled him over and over and he was in a badly exhausted state when at last he set foot on the damp sand of the shore. In the pitch blackness he staggered through the gale and showers of rain and sleet until he met a man called Rimmer who helped him to his home. Rimmer then rushed to Birkdale Police Station to raise the alarm. John Jackson also managed to struggle ashore but in the darkness he was not seen by anyone. It was not until he arrived at his own house after staggering and sometimes crawling that he received assistance. Both men had been too exhausted and dazed to try to help any of their companions even if they could have found them in the storm.

St. Annes lifeboat 'Laura Janet' launching

The St. Annes Lifeboat '*Laura Janet*' had been launched at around 10.25 p.m. through the surf crashing on the beach, and was rowed for about 500 yards before the sails were set as she crossed Salthouse Bank. She was not seen after this, and what happened to her can only be supposition as nobody returned to tell the tale. The '*Laura Janet*' capsized and appears to have failed to right herself. Two red lights and other signals were noticed about two miles offshore from Southport during that fateful night and may have indicated she was in trouble but that is uncertain.

As the grey dawn light spread over the desolate landscape rumours started to circulate in St. Annes that the '*Laura Janet*' had safely arrived up the coast at Fleetwood but they were soon proved to be proved false. At 9.30 a.m. the worst was presumed and a messenger was sent to Lytham. The crew of the '*Charles Biggs*' had gone to bed but when summoned to search for the St. Annes boat they agreed without hesitation to go. Within the hour the Lytham Lifeboat '*Charles Biggs*', with the same crew that had been on-board the lifeboat the night before, was launched to commence a search. The wind had moderated by dawn and the search began along the south side of the River Ribble towards the Southport shore.

Up-turned Southport lifeboat 'Eliza Fernley' on shoreline

At Southport the wrecked hull of the Southport life-boat *'Eliza Fernley'* had been located on the shoreline, yet in mourning the loss of their boat and most of the crew they still did not realise that the St. Annes boat was missing that morning, until a few minutes before noon when the Lytham Lifeboat *'Charles Biggs'* came alongside the pier and explained that they were looking for her. A search of the shoreline was commenced and around 1.00 p.m. someone with a telescope made out a white outline in the sea. When they reached the spot they found it was the upturned hull of the 'Laura Janet' lifeboat. No-one was found alive but three bodies were found entangled beneath the hull. One of them had a silver pocket watch that had stopped at 2.30 a.m. and it was presumed that this was the time when something catastrophic happened to the lifeboat.

Illustration of the Southport Disaster in The Graphic 18th December, 1886.

The national press carried illustrated newspaper reports depicting the scene and loss of life. This was national news in the Illustrated London Newspaper and The Graphic with lithographic illustration. Twelve men had been saved from the Mexico by the Lytham Lifeboat, but of the 44 men who set out in the three lifeboats from Southport, St. Annes and

Lytham 27 were lost, leaving 16 widows and 50 orphans.

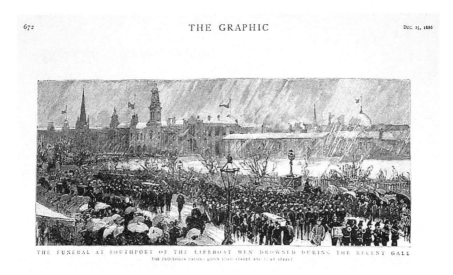

672   THE GRAPHIC   Dec. 25, 1886

THE FUNERAL AT SOUTHPORT OF THE LIFEBOAT MEN DROWNED DURING THE RECENT GALE
THE PROCESSION PASSING DOWN LORD STREET AND QUEEN STREET

The funerals at Southport depicted in The Graphic 25th December, 1886.

The funerals in Southport were a big event but note the date on the illustration. This was Christmas week and the outpouring of grief was magnified by the closeness to Christmas, in much the same way as when the Penlee lifeboat Solomon Brown was lost in a disaster more recently in Christmas week on the 19th December 1981.

The main reason for the great demand for a place on the Lifeboat was undoubtedly poverty, as it was winter time and the fishermen were unable to go to sea and there was no money coming in. The fishermen who formed the majority of the crew had fallen on lean times, and, for the most part were in great need. In particular, the poor circumstances of the fishermen at that time were due to the scarcity of shrimps that were the local catch. Also in the summer season the Southport fishermen hired out their boats for pleasure sails at the Pierhead, hoping to make surplus money to see them through the Winter, but the previous two summers had been poor weather, with little opportunity for pleasure trips.

The reward of a sovereign ($£1$) for going out on the lifeboat was therefore an attraction surpassing the risks involved. In fact one of the crew had been advised not to step forward as he was a man *'pretty well to do'* as the owner of a Greengrocers shop and his going out would prevent one of the other men from earning a sovereign.

H. ROBINSON.(saved)	Wreck of the "Mexico."	J. JACKSON, (saved)
R.PETERS.2nd Coxwain	C. HODGE, Coxwain.	B. PETERS.
T. JACKSON.	T. RIGBY.	P. WRIGHT.
T. SPENCER.	H. HODGE.	H. RIGBY.

Eleven of the sixteen crew members of the Southport lifeboat *Eliza Fernley*

But what of the human impact on the households of those who died?

Peter Wright

Peter Wright was a 24 year old fisherman nicknamed *'Diamond'* on the Southport lifeboat crew. He was found under the lifeboat entangled in the ropes. He left a widow, who on hearing of her husband's tragic death went into premature labour and gave birth to a still-born child. Peter and his still born child were laid to rest in the same coffin.

Thomas Jackson - was a 27 year old fisherman who volunteered for the Southport lifeboat. He left a widow and two children – the oldest aged four years and another aged 10 weeks. He and his family lived in the same house as Timothy Rigby and his family with his wife and four children aged four years down to 1 week old.

Thomas Jackson   Timothy Rigby

Timothy's body was found with Peter Wright's also entangled under the lifeboat. Jackson's widow was utterly helpless, having no means of support. She did not have any relatives in Southport and the family was in the deepest poverty, finding it difficult to get sufficient money to buy bread. On the previous Monday, Jackson had gone to sea and managed to catch a few quarts of shrimps, which he then sold to a fish merchant. It was customary for the fishermen to be paid at the end of the week, but Jackson was obliged to go for his money on Wednesday night, to buy a loaf of bread for his family.

John Jackson (saved)

The day before he went out in the lifeboat he had no provisions of any kind in his house, except dried bread. He was the brother of John Jackson, one of the survivors from the Southport lifeboat.

John Jackson was one of the survivors, who managed to get ashore and walked home crawling and staggering. As a survivor his accounts were invaluable in understanding the circumstances of the loss of the Southport lifeboat and most of its crew. He was unfit to give evidence at the Inquest as he had undergone surgery recently. It was said of John Jackson that he would never speak of his heroism.

From the age of 16 to 50 he was a member of the lifeboat crew and 'made it an honourable boast that he never missed a lifeboat practice'. Three of his sons, and a son-in-law were members of the lifeboat crew at the time of his death at 70 years of age.

John Jackson

Henry Robinson was previously mentioned as a survivor from under the hull of the capsized lifeboat. His account at the inquest gave tremendous insight into the events of the night of the Mexico incident.

Henry Robinson (saved)   Henry Robinson

St. Annes lifeboat '*Laura Janet*' and crew

No equivalent crew images exist for the St. Annes lifeboat crew of the *Laura Janet*, whose crew were all lost. The body of 35 year old Thomas Bonney – one of the crew members pictured here was the last to be recovered some 3 months later in March 1887. It was so badly decomposed that he was only identified by a local cobbler, who recognised the repairs to Bonney's boots. He was married and the father of five children. It is said that his only sustenance all day had been a basin of gruel, and that he was therefore ill equipped for the ordeal of that fateful night. It was stated that he stinted himself for the sake of his family and that his children had always appeared to be well fed and clothed. His relation James Bonney, aged 21 years, and of the same address had also died in the St Anne's Lifeboat leaving a widow and one child.

Hull of Mexico on Southport beach

The hull of the Mexico remained on the sands off Southport beach. The cargo was removed and 3 months later, with the aid of two Preston tugs, the hull was eventually floated up the River Ribble to Lytham where she remained for the next 2 years as a show ship attracting visitors. An irony of this incident is that if the crew of the Mexico had remained with their vessel they would have been safe as the iron hull came to rest on the flat sandy bottom, but that view is only with the benefit of hindsight and on that fateful night every effort was being made to save life from shipwreck. This wasn't the end of the Mexico. After her two year stay at Lytham she was repaired, re-rigged and sold again to a Danish firm. She made one voyage to the Falkland Islands before being sold to a Norwegian firm and with a new name 'Valhalla' she set out from London to Dundee, only to become a total loss off Tantallon on the north-east coast of Scotland in 1900.

A considerable amount of money was collected in Germany to aid the bereaved relatives of the lifeboatmen who lost their lives attempting the rescue from the ill-fated barque Mexico. Some £900 was apportioned to

Lifeboat monument in St. Annes

St.Annes and £700 to Southport. Of the £1,600 donated £250 had been given by the Emperor of Germany himself; some £1,300 from the citizens of Hamburg – the home port of the Mexico, and a further sum from the German residents of Liverpool.

A monument was erected by public subscription in memory of those who were lost.

The disaster of 1886 had far-reaching consequences for R.N.L.I. fund-raising. Among the residents of St.Annes at the time lived a wealthy Manchester businessman Charles Macara. He believed the quiet seaside town was a good bolt-hole from the pressures of Victorian enterprise.

He enjoyed the company and rough conversation of local fishermen in the taverns and even went out with them on fishing trips. During the incident of the loss of the two lifeboats he found himself involved in communication with other towns as he had the only telephone in St.Annes at that time. When the scale of the disaster was understood he shared the despair of those around him and resolved to make a difference.

Lifeboat Saturday 17th October, 1891 - parade through streets of Salford and Manchester

As he investigated the R.N.L.I. finances he discovered that only a relatively small number of rich philanthropists – about 100 - were keeping the finances afloat. Convinced that fund-raising should be done in the wider population he made a bold plan for persuading people to contribute. He began with an appeal to the press. By the autumn of 1891 the first ever Lifeboat Saturday was held, when two reserve lifeboats and their crews were pulled on carriages through the streets of Manchester and Salford for two days before its inauguration. On the Saturday of the parade, life-boatmen in the boats held long poles with nets attached so they could reach up to receive donations from high windows and the top decks of trams and buses. The boats were accompanied by a large group of women collectors rattling tins at ground level. The idea of Lifeboat Saturday quickly spread and by 1893 it had become a feature of British life. It raised the annual average of income for the R.N.L.I. to around £40,000, thereby making it possible to increase the lifeboat fleet and the remuneration of the crews.

Early financial support for the newly founded Lifeboat Institution came from individual subscription and the major donations came from no more than around 100 people. Following the Mexico disaster financial help for the dependents of the St. Anne's and Southport lifeboat crew was urgently needed, and thanks to Lord Derby's patronage further funding and a structure for long-term distribution of the monies was put in place.

Charles was supported in his fund-raising by his wife Marion who knew from experiencing the St. Anne's disaster at first hand the agonies of those waiting on shore for the safe return of a lifeboat crew.

Although Charles had planned the Lifeboat Saturday appeal in Manchester, it was his wife who secured the support of the Mayoress of Manchester and took the initiative in organising fund-raising committees in Manchester and Salford. Using her considerable organising skills and using emotive language and rhetoric Marion Macara had begun what was to become the Ladies' Lifeboat Auxiliary, with aspirations for branches in every county, city, and town. While Lifeboat Saturday became established as an annual fund-raising event across the United Kingdom the ladies were more imaginative and resourceful, linking the pleasure of social events such as concerts, balls, garden parties and afternoon teas with fund-raising. Marion Macara's strategy of engaging influential ladies in local communities worked well and in many towns it became a signal of social acceptability and privilege to be invited to join the lifeboat committee.

During the First World War years the committees continued as best they could but these were difficult times to fund-raise. In 1921 to give renewed impetus to fund-raising the Ladies Lifeboat Guild was formed; with HRH the Prince of Wales at the annual meeting. The basic idea was to improve the co-ordination of the committees and provide better support. The Ladies Lifeboat Guild was inaugurated at a meeting in Claridges Hotel, London in June 1921, with all Presidents and Secretaries invited from committees throughout the country. The Duchess of Portland, who had a long record of supporting the Lifeboat Ladies Auxiliary, became the first President. It was the new Guild that began the campaign of house to house envelope collections. Civic support continued to be important in establishing the position of the local Ladies Lifeboat Guild at the heart of the social community. The centenary of the R.N.L.I in 1924 was celebrated throughout the nation and the Ladies Guilds were encouraged to raise funds through lifeboat demonstrations, carnivals, dinners and balls.

As in the previous war the Second World War led to fewer fund-raising events but they were still an important source of income to keep the lifeboats operating at a time of great demand on their services. Huge societal changes took place in the post war years that put pressure on the Lifeboat Institution, both operationally and financially. With ambitious plans to expand and modernise the fleet, and with funding reserves running low, the Lifeboat Guilds were encouraged to increase their efforts. The appeal to the Ladies Lifeboat Guilds' was met with an overwhelming response as many volunteers found the alternative of Government support unacceptable for a service that had for so long prided itself on its voluntary status. Collections around public houses and clubs linked to Lifeboat Day were well supported by members of the public.

The loss of a lifeboat and its crew is always a sad, and thankfully rare, event but when the entire crew of eight men were lost from the Longhope Lifeboat in Orkney capsized on service in March 1969 the public response in donations to the lifeboat service was impressive. When in December 1981 and just six days before Christmas the Penlee lifeboat was lost with its eight crew members, whilst on service to rescue the crew of the coaster Union Star. The national outpouring of grief and sympathy for the eight families in the community of the villages of Mousehole, Cornwall was accompanied by considerable increase in public donations as this incident touched and motivated the public to do their bit to contribute to the lifeboat service.

Legacy gifts and bequests from wills have formed an important element of lifeboat funding for over a century. Many individuals who lost a family member in the conflicts of the First and Second World Wars, or in remembrance of their time served in the Navy during hostilities and left money in their will to the R.N.L.I. to build a lifeboat that would carry the name of the person they wanted to commemorate. Such legacies have been an important funding stream over the decades and it is calculated that six out of every ten lifeboat launches are funded through such bequests.

Kay Hurley was brought up in Yorkshire but lived her adult life in London. Following the incident on the River Thames with the pleasure cruiser 'Marchioness' in 1998, in which many young lives were lost, she decided that she would provide funding for a lifeboat for London on the River Thames. She was pleased to discover that plans were already being implemented for a lifeboat station on the Thames but disappointed to learn that the lifeboats had already been funded. However, she was told of a separate initiative to develop and deploy hovercraft at appropriate stations. Such locations typically have vast areas of sandbanks, mudflats, and muddy estuaries that dry out at low water and are covered at high water, and where conditions are difficult for traditional inshore lifeboats to operate.

When she was asked to consider funding one of these hovercraft, Kay had never seen such a craft that effectively flies over the mud on a cushion of air. Being a Yorkshire woman she wanted to know that her money was being well spent, and when she was taken to see one of these craft operate in Poole Harbour she was impressed and committed to funding a hovercraft. She also knew that her Australian husband would have approved of this gift, as he had been a keen oarsman, regularly rowing on the Thames. The hovercraft that she funded was to be stationed at Morecambe in Lancashire, where there are rising tides, and dangerous mud flats, including quicksand. Her next task was to choose its name in readiness for the naming ceremony in December 2002. Using her surname, and in recognition of its fast speed she named it the *'Hurley Flyer'*. Never was such a craft in the right place at the right time, in the hands of competent lifesavers, than on the night of the 5th February 2004. The *Hurley Flyer* was deployed, along with other rescue services including helicopters and coastguard teams, to go to the assistance of over thirty Chinese 'Cockle-picker' fishermen. They had ventured out onto the treacherous sandbanks of Morecambe Bay at the wrong state of tide/ and were caught unawares by the fast incoming tides when in darkness they were gathering cockles. The illegal profiteering gang-masters had paid insufficient notice to the tide-tables, putting their workers in mortal danger. The Chinese workers had no safety equipment and no knowledge of the area they had been brought to for work on that fateful night. The bad weather conditions were exacerbated by heavy downfalls of rain in previous days in the Lake District draining large quantities of freshwater into the Bay and this freshwater was even colder in February than the seawater in Morecambe Bay. Some men were plucked from the icy waters naked as, in desperation, they had discarded their clothing to attempt to swim to safety. Twenty one bodies of men and women were recovered from the Bay. The majority were young men in their 20's and 30's, along with two women. A further body was recovered in 2010. Fourteen other members of the group were reported to have made it to the shore, making fifteen survivors in total.

The R.N.L.I. defines itself proudly, simply and accurately as the 'Charity that saves lives at sea'. Yet there are times such as the Morecambe Bay Cockle Pickers disaster, thankfully rare, when the challenge is beyond any crew; where skill and courage alone will never be sufficient enough to overcome the odds.

5 THE LIFE-BOATS

The mandate and commission of the R.N.L.I has for many years been to respond to maritime incidents up to 50 miles from the shores of the UK, and the geographic dispersion of life-boat stations with offshore life-boats capable of operating as a 50 mile service range has met that requirement for over a century. Throughout its history the R.N.L.I. has kept abreast of technology innovations, especially in hull design, propulsion systems, and nowadays electronics, whilst balancing the adoption of new technology with the essential requirement for reliability, especially in the hostile salt-water rough sea environment that life-boats operate in. More recently that commitment has increased to 100 miles from shore and to increase the service range of offshore life-boats a plan is being implemented in the twenty first century to develop a life-boat capable of higher speed of around 25 knots. This gives a capability to respond to incidents at that increased range in an acceptable time.

A sub-title for this chapter could have been 'Lifeboat design and technology has come a long way in the past 100 years'. This applies not only to lifeboat hull design, construction materials, propulsion systems, but also communication systems and electronic navigational aids. The early lifeboats of the R.N.L.I. were either rowing, or rowing and sailing lifeboats as these forms of propulsion were tried and tested even in extreme weather conditions.

In the mid nineteenth century steam power was the cutting edge of technology in the mid-nineteenth century, because it was steam engines that were increasingly being used to drive paddles or screw propellers for ship propulsion. However, steam engines were prone to breakdown and it was the need for reliability in the violent moods of the sea that held back the use of steam engines in lifeboats. Lifeboats needed to be able to withstand the tossing around in rough seas when salt water could be sweeping over the entire lifeboat.

On shore steam engines were powering textile mills, metal foundries and railways, driving the development of the Industrial Revolution in replacing wind and water-mill power.

The first idea for a steam lifeboat came from the fertile mind of Sir William Hillary in 1824 (quite early in lifeboat history), who published a plan for the construction of a steam lifeboat, yet it was 1886 before the first steam lifeboat was brought into service. To get a workable engine the boat had to be longer in order to carry sufficient fresh water to feed the boiler, and fuel for the boiler fire-box, and was therefore heavier than most lifeboats

Steam lifeboat circa 1886

and this meant they had to remain afloat all the time. The risks of fire in a wooden hull vessel with a coal fired boiler that was expected to operate in rough sea conditions were considered too great. The combined issues of lack of reliability, high risk of fire and the large physical size of a steam propelled lifeboat caused a reticence in deploying steam technology as it restricted the stations that could take one of these larger craft. It was 1889 before the R.N.L.I. took delivery of its first steam powered lifeboat and in the interim years of increasing numbers of commercial steam vessels there was an increasing dependency of rowing and sailing lifeboats on using steam powered harbour tugs to tow the lifeboat to get the lifeboat to the scene of an incident faster than may have otherwise been possible.

The 1820's were the beginning of the age of steam navigation when William Hillary was minded to adopt this new propulsion technology of steam power, and a screw propeller. They were also the heyday of the sailing ship, which was making great strides forward in naval architecture and ship design. This allowed new heights of achievement in size, speed, efficiency, and above all else in the beauty of such ships as the clippers such as Cutty Sark and the Royal Navy Blackwall frigates that were at the peak of development.

Sailing ships owed nothing to the Industrial Revolution and those who designed and built them wanted nothing to do with steam navigation. They

built beautifully using the finest hardwoods in the world and a great schism arose between those who believed in sailing ships and loved them and those who had committed themselves and their future to steam. Yet men like Brunel went on building their smoking funnelled vessels, making them larger and larger and

'A great schism arose between sail and steam'

with increasingly powerful engines.

Steam tug Wardleys towing Maude Pickup lifeboat   Courtesy Fleetwood Museum

However, few steam lifeboats were introduced into the R.N.L.I. for the reasons outlined above. Remarkably the practice of tug boats towing lifeboats continued around the coast until motor lifeboats replaced the earlier pulling and sailing lifeboats. This painting is of the Fleetwood Lifeboat Maude Pickup that was stationed at Fleetwood from 1894 until 1930. The tried and tested ancient system of rowing and sailing life-boats continued to be the propulsion system of choice for life-boats until the early decades of the twentieth century.

It was the tragic loss of the passenger vessel Rohilla on rocks off Whitby, on the East Yorkshire coast, and a rescue that lasted over three days that confirmed the essential need to use motor lifeboats. The Rohilla was a passenger vessel converted to a hospital ship during the First World War when on 30th October 1914 in the blackout conditions of no navigational aids of lighthouses or buoys she foundered near Whitby and quickly broke in half. Two rowing lifeboats from Whitby immediately launched when the distress signals were seen, but due to the rocks they were unable to get alongside the Rohilla and one lifeboat was damaged beyond repair. Other lifeboats from Scarborough and Teesmouth were summoned but when they arrived they were unable to get to the Rohilla either then or the next day.

Hospital ship *Rohilla* wrecked off Whitby

Rowing lifeboats had simply not got the power to get to the wreck - close in to the shore as it was, and there was considerable loss of life. After successive attempts over more than a day it was apparent that only a motor lifeboat had any chance of approaching the wreck. The Tynemouth motor lifeboat was summoned and immediately undertook the 44 mile nightmarish journey in total darkness through the storm.

Crew and medical staff had been trapped on board the wrecked hull for 2 days as unsuccessful attempts were made by rocket line apparatus and lifeboats. It was the use of the newly motorised Tynemouth lifeboat that effected a rescue of 50 people after three days. Gold medals were awarded to the coxswains of the Whitby No. 2 and Tynemouth lifeboats, and Silver medals to the second coxswains of these boats.

Just as steam traction engines on land were rapidly being replaced by petrol engine tractors, so the introduction of steam lifeboats was rapidly eclipsed by the replacement of steam engines with petrol motors in lifeboats.

However, both steam and petrol engines were seen by lifeboat crews' as being prone to breakdown for many years were seen as an auxiliary means of propulsion to the oars and sail. A problem to resolve with the coming of the petrol engine was how to enclose the engine in a watertight compartment that could allow sufficient air circulation to both feed this air aspirated engine and cool it.

The Anne Letitia Russell was the lifeboat I served on as a junior crew member. She was 41 feet long and had twin Parsons Porbeagle 47 horse power diesel engine, giving a maximum speed of just over 8 knots, about twice walking pace, but she could maintain that speed in all weathers. The only instruments on board were a compass, depth sounder, and a radio transmitter and receiver. She was not self-righting – which may surprise many people but she was an excellent sea-boat, a thorough-bred, and we had pride in her and she was kind on her crew. It was a fantastic feeling to be on a safe platform in bad weather, even though she was a wet boat with little shelter for the crew by modern day standards, being just huddled under the wooden canopy or standing on the open side-decks. In bad weather it was the norm to get wet rather than nowadays being strapped inside a warm dry cabin in a cushion padded seat; but the expectation was to get wet and although we cursed as the water ran down our necks inside the oilskin jackets, we simply didn't know any different and were glad that at least we didn't have to row the boat as former lifeboat crews had to do.

Fleetwood Lifeboat Service
Boards

It was only in researching the background to put together these chapters that I realised a new perspective on my time in the R.N.L.I. and the scrutiny of the service boards made me think. The Fleetwood Lifeboat service boards show that it was 1933 before a motor lifeboat arrived and the Anne Letitia Russell lifeboat was sent to the station in 1939.

When I volunteered for the lifeboat in 1967 it was less than 4 decades since the lifeboat had been of the pulling and sailing type. (I simply didn't feel that at the time and pulling and sailing lifeboats seemed like ancient history when I was a crew member of the Anne Letitia Russell).

The Anne Letitia Russell Watson lifeboat was stationed at Fleetwood for 37 years and replaced in 1976 by a Waveney class lifeboat 'Lady of Lancashire'. She was a revolutionary departure from the traditional hull design of the former Watson and Oakley classes of lifeboats. The 44 foot hull shape was based on an American Coastguard cutter design, and powered by twin 260 horse power General Motors engines giving a speed of 16 knots - twice as fast as her predecessor. Her hull design with the raised main and rear cabin gave her self-righting properties but with exposed propeller shafts to give the increased speed she was not suitable for slipway launching and she remained permanently afloat in a small open dock tied to a floating pontoon. The increased speed was a remarkable transformation, and now the lifeboat was fitted with radar.

Waveney Class Fleetwood Lifeboat 'Lady of Lancashire'

This picture was taken from a gas rig support vessel in 1985 as the life-boat headed West with me in command on that day to the aid of a disabled yacht some 20 miles off Fleetwood, beyond the new Offshore Gas platforms in Morecambe Bay Gas Field.

In the era of lifeboats such as the Ann Letitia Russell all-night searches often happened because vessels that were in difficulty, often due to engine failure, may have been unable to communicate with the shore. The introduction of radar, complemented by improved communication, including VHF Direction finders meant it became easier to locate vessels in the darkness, thereby reducing the number of all-night searches.

Tyne Class lifeboat *William Street'*

Thirteen years later In 1989 the Lady of Lancashire lifeboat was replaced by a Tyne Class lifeboat William Street. Slightly longer at 47 feet and with twin General Motors engines she had an even faster speed of 18 knots. She was built at Cowes on the Isle of Wight and in Summer 1989 I spent a week along the south coast partaking in the finishing trials. Now with two steering positions, one inside the cabin and a second one outside she was fitted with advanced communications equipment, the latest colour radar, direction finding systems, and electronic position fixing kit. The William Street has remained on station at Fleetwood for the past 25 years, and is replaced by the latest Shannon Class lifeboat in Spring 2016.

An innovation in the early 1960's was the Inshore lifeboat, just 16 feet long,

Fleetwood Inshore Lifeboat with Stephen Musgrave at the helm and Dave Owen as crew.

powered by a 40 horse power outboard engine, giving a speed of around 22 knots. This was a major development as a lifeboat that was quick to launch and capable of operating in shallow waters.

These have evolved to become the rigid inflatable fast inshore lifeboats such as this one stationed along the coast at Blackpool.

Rigid Inflatable Inshore Lifeboat.

Morecambe hovercraft *'Hurley Flyer'*

The R.N.L.I. continues to push boundaries of technology innovation and without the 'Hurley Flyer' hovercraft stationed at Morecambe when the Chinese cockle pickers met their fate on the sands of Morecambe Bay in February 2004 it is arguable that the death toll may have been higher.

The Shannon class lifeboat is the first all-weather lifeboat propelled by water-jets instead of propellers, making it the most agile and manoeuvrable all-weather lifeboat in the fleet. Measuring just 13 metres long it is capable of 25 knots. The Waveney and Tyne class lifeboats previously at Fleetwood had Corten steel hulls, and the predecessor Watson lifeboat Anne Letitia Russell was a wooden hull. The new Shannon class lifeboat is made of a composite material consisting of glass and some carbon fibre. She is designed to operate safely in waves up to 16 metres.

The innovations of the revolutionary design of the Shannon class lifeboat are it's plastic hull and water-jet propulsion This vessel is fitted with the latest technology including computerised systems information management, enabling monitoring of temperatures and pressure data from any seated crew position, along with advanced electronic navigation and communication equipment as a fast offshore lifeboat. The R.N.L.I. has a building programme to construct these boats in its own boat construction yard at Littlehampton.

Evolution in technology has not only transformed the life-boats themselves. The traditional method of assembling the lifeboat crew was to fire two maroons. These were basically firework mortars that sent an explosive charge high into the air, giving a cannon like explosion when the charge detonated in the sky. Two of these maroons were fired as signals, both to alert the lifeboat crew that there services were needed, and also as a reply signal in response to the distress call to the individuals who had called upon the lifeboat service. The use of explosive signals follows the naval tradition from the 19th century of firing a cannon on entering a port to indicate the presence of their ship and confirm its peaceful intentions in discharging their weapon. The shore battery would respond with three blasts to welcome the ship to the port. The R.N.L.I. has used explosive maroons for around 150 years as an assembly signal to summon the crew to the lifeboat station. Two maroons were used as a confirmation signal in case the first explosion had been misheard. In the 1960's when Inshore Lifeboats were introduced into the lifeboat service the practice of firing a single maroon was used to differentiate between the call being for the offshore lifeboat (2 maroons) or the inshore lifeboat (1 maroon). The maroons used for the inshore lifeboat were generally smaller 'Icarus' rockets that weren't as loud as the mortar maroons for the offshore lifeboat. Since around 1985 electronic 'pagers' have been introduced and now used as a replacement for the explosive maroons.

What of the future in another 100 years? A fact is that the Shannon Lifeboat is designed to remain in the fleet for 50 years, doubling the current life expectancy of a lifeboat hull.

6 OTHER INCIDENTS

The motor lifeboat Ann Letitia Russell was placed on station at Fleetwood in February 1939. and early in the Second World War in October 1941 in black-out conditions of no lights on navigational buoys or lighthouses this lifeboat and its crew were called upon to undertake a service in extreme weather conditions, and for which coxswain Jeffrey Wright and Station Mechanic Syd Hill were awarded the Silver Medal of the R.N.L.I. for rescuing the eight crew members of a Faroese Schooner that had grounded on the King Scar sandbank some two miles from Fleetwood Promenade.

Stella Marie - In August 1941 the three masted schooner Stella Marie, of Thorshaven, had sailed for Fleetwood with a full cargo of fish for the

Stella Marie heading for Fleetwood

port. The port of Thorshaven is in the Faroe Islands that lie beyond the Orkney and Shetland Islands and half way to the Norwegian coast. On entering the approaches of Morecambe Bay on August 5th, 1941, in deteriorating weather conditions that were already of gale force from the North West

they had to anchor to wait for high water and a pilot to take her into the harbour. During the day the wind increased to severe gale force 9 from the NorthNorthWest, and the anchor started to drag. In attempting to raise the dragging anchor it became fouled and due to the strain of heaving the anchor in with the hull pitching up and down in heavy seas the anchor cable parted leaving the Stella Marie drifting towards the sandbanks. The captain accepted the offer of a tow from a tug, but in atrocious weather conditions the towing hawser parted, and with the vessel being driven towards King Scar the lifeboat was summoned from Fleetwood.

Realising their difficulty, and unable to launch the ship's boat, in the appalling conditions the crew climbed the rigging and lashed themselves to the shrouds as the vessel approached the breaking surf on the rapidly approaching shoreline. The lifeboat experienced large waves on the bow as it headed North West into the wind slowing their progress.

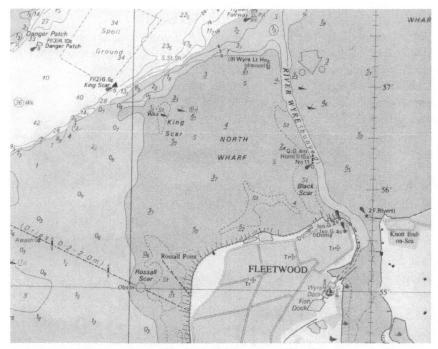

Chart of Fleetwood and King Scar sandbank where Stella Marie was wrecked in 1941

The Stella Marie was in shoal water aground on King Scar when coxswain Jeff Wright arrived with his crew at the Stella Marie.

Quickly assessing the situation he realised that he would be unable to approach from the leeward side and would have to risk coming in from the windward side to place the lifeboat alongside the stricken vessel.

Large waves and breaking surf washed over the lifeboat, flooding the cockpit at one stage, and crashing the Ann Letitia Russell lifeboat alongside the Stella Marie with exceptional force. In getting alongside the Stella Marie the lifeboat struck the sandy bottom on King Scar with such force that the rudder (that is lowerable when the lifeboat is at sea and raised for re-housing in the lifeboathouse) was forced to the top of its steel pintle bending and jamming the rudder mechanism making the lifeboat difficult to steer, but the coxswain was able to hold the lifeboat alongside long enough for the eight crew of the Stella Marie to be pulled onto the lifeboat.

Fleetwood lifeboat arriving alongside Stella Marie

Using the engines to help steer the lifeboat, and despite the jammed rudder, the coxswain was able to put the engines astern and reverse away from the stricken hull of the Stella Marie.

In doing this and with waves breaking over the stern of the lifeboat as it reversed away the mechanic Syd Hill was at times up to his neck in water operating the engine controls down in the cockpit.

Heavy seas breaking over lifeboat hampered the rescue

For this rescue coxswain Jeff Wright and Mechanic Syd Hill were awarded the Silver medal and each of the other four members of the crew, including Dick 'Cush' Wright who was the Assistant Mechanic received the 'Thanks of the Institution' on an illuminated Vellum for their part in this outstanding service.

The wreck remained on King Scar broken backed until the sea broke it up. Wreckage from the Stella Marie, in particular the engine block and windlass were visible from Fleetwood Promenade for decades after this incident. For more than 35 years the annual 'Wreck Trek' takes hundreds of people as a guided party across the sands, when the spring tides are right and approaching low water, as a fund-raising activity for the R.N.L.I., visiting the site of the Stella Marie on King Scar and passing Wyre Light and a number of other wreck locations.

Stella Marie aground and broken backed on King Scar

Yacht Setantii 30th August, 1982 - Weekends, and especially Bank Holiday weekends are a time when many people go to sea for pleasure, and also a time when many calls are made on the lifeboat service. It is often the case when people are time limited in their long weekend break and need to get back home to go to work the next day that incidents occur. Disregarding adverse weather forecasts because of other life pressures is reckless and has its consequences that can become life-threatening, if not fatal. In the case of the yacht Setantii in 1982 the Fleetwood offshore lifeboat 'Lady of Lancashire' was launched at 18.30 p.m. on August 30th 1982 (Bank Holiday

Fleetwood lifeboat 'Lady of Lancashire'

weekend) following a report of distress flares sighted off the Blackpool coast. It was believed likely to be the Setantii a 25 foot yacht reported overdue in sailing from the Isle of Man, some 60 miles away. The lifeboat proceeded in bad weather to a reported position 3 miles West of Blackpool Tower. The winds were gale force 8 from the North West and the seas were very rough. Traditionally this is the start of the Illuminations season in Blackpool and around this time equinoctial gales often cause bad weather with strong winds and stormy conditions. No radio contact was made at all despite repeated calls, and in the rough seas progress was relatively slow. Approximately 45 minutes after launching and still in daylight a mast and sail was sighted and the lifeboat was steered toward the casualty.

I was deputy coxswain for this job and as we approached we couldn't quite believe what we were witnessing. Only one person was observed on board the yacht Setantii but two others were being dragged through the water behind the yacht, attached by their lifelines. A small storm sail was keeping Setantii moving through the water but despite his efforts the single person on board the yacht was unable to drag the two people who had been washed overboard back on to the yacht.

Two crew from Setantii trailing over stern as lifeboat approaches

In talking to the Setantii crew after this incident, and they all survived, they had been in the Isle of Man for the Bank Holiday weekend and were returning to Fleetwood in Morecambe Bay even though the weather was a bad forecast. With the wind from the North West it was blowing from behind them and didn't seem too bad, but with reduced visibility the first landmark they saw was Blackpool Tower and they immediately realised they were too far south. It was when they turned round to head North and into the seas that they got into difficulty, with cresting waves breaking right over their boat.

The sole member of the yacht's crew on board Setantii was clearly exhausted when we arrived alongside the yacht with the life-boat and tried to pass a rope across; he was too weak to assist in tying the rope to the yacht. It was therefore necessary to put one of the lifeboat crew on board Setantii to secure the tow rope.

Knowing the character and capability of your lifeboat crew colleagues is essential and never more than in bad weather when difficult tasks have to be carried out. In such a situation I would never ask a lifeboat colleague to attempt a task that I wouldn't be prepared to do myself. On this task a lifeboat crew member called Dave Bolland was a stalwart seaman, who during his national service in the Army had volunteered for the Parachute Regiment. A plumber by trade he was a dependable person who would jump when asked to jump and in this case I needed him to jump across to the deck of the Setantii with a rope from the lifeboat and assist the yacht crew.

As deputy coxswain I briefed Dave on what was needed – to put one of our crew on board Setantii and secure a tow rope to enable the lifeboat to control and arrest the motion of Setantii, then to rapidly recover the two yachtsmen who were in the sea, trailing behind Setantii. The plan was to get them back on their own boat and then transfer them across to the lifeboat, having tied the yacht's steering tiller in a mid-ships position.

Setantii under tow by Fleetwood lifeboat

The whole task was carried out quickly with Dave jumping across to Setantii carrying a 'heaving line' attached at one end to the lifeboat tow rope. Using this line the lifeboat tow rope was then dragged across to

Setantii and made fast at the front of the yacht. The yacht's sail was released and the lifeboat then held the yacht into the wind in a stationary position to enable the yacht crew to be plucked from the sea.

The job of the lifeboat is to save lives, and not property but when the yacht's crew members were brought on board, along with lifeboat crewman Dave, the crew of Setantii collectively implored us to save their boat as they had valuable belongings on board. We discussed this option and agreed that we would attempt a tow back to Fleetwood. The wind at this point was still gale force 8. Many modern yacht's do not have adequate towing points on the bow front of the vessel and I had instructed crewman Dave to tie the rope both at the front bow fastening and also to take the rope around the base of the mast and secure it to the sail 'sheet' winches near the back of the boat as these are a strong-point fastening.

Setantii bow cleat shears and pulpit breaks off

The tow was commenced at slow speed but within 5 minutes a large wave struck Setantii – the tow rope went tight and suddenly the bow fastening on the yacht failed and the force of this broke off the pulpit rail from the front.

Tow rope around mast pulls Setantii's mast down

The tow rope was still connected to the lifeboat but the tow-rope fastening point was now around the base of the mast. The consequence was that Setantii was now towing badly, veering wildly from one side to the other and predictably within a minute or two the mast came tumbling down, along with all the wire rigging. This was a big problem and the decision was about to be taken by the coxswain and crew when again the Setantii yacht skipper pleaded with us to try to save his vessel.

The rope around the yacht's mast stump soon slipped off, worsening the situation, but the tow rope was still connecting the lifeboat to the sail winches in the cockpit of the yacht. The lifeboat's engines were stopped to enable a review of the situation. The lifeboat coxswain did not want to approach the Setantii because the mast and rigging were in the water, as a hazard that could foul the lifeboat propellers if we tried to recover the tow rope and release Setantii to its fate. When the engines were put into gear again the yacht began towing backwards – stern first behind the lifeboat.

Setantii hull towing stern first behind lifeboat

The weather was very rough but the yacht crew members who had been in the water had warmed up and they desperately wanted us to do our utmost to save their yacht so we continued to proceed back to the lifeboat station with the yacht hull towing astern – the mast and rigging trailing behind it – and the trailing rigging actually helping with keeping the yacht in a straight line.

All seemed to be going well and the yacht remained in tow behind the lifeboat at slow speed for more than an hour. However, just two miles from the lifeboat station and in darkness now at the top of the Fleetwood Channel the tow parted. A container ferry was entering Morecambe Bay inward bound for the Fleetwood Channel, and Setantii as a floating obstruction at the top of the main shipping channel was effectively a hazard to shipping that would close the port until it was removed from the channel.

Setantii tow rope parts

Conditions were still bad, and arguably worse. In hasty discussion with the coxswain, and having already mentioned that I wouldn't ask any of the crew to undertake a task that I would not be prepared to do myself, I decided that as I had a better knowledge of yachts and sailing boats I would go across to the yacht, taking the rope with me. The coxswain manoeuvred the yacht alongside and I jumped on board Setantii with the rope. The seas were short and steep around the channel entrance and with difficulty I re-attached the rope to the yacht around the only strong point fastening that were the sail sheet winches. I then had to get myself back on board the lifeboat.

I assessed the situation as the coxswain manoeuvred the lifeboat into position alongside the yacht to get me back on board but as I waited for the opportunity to get across and judged the best moment to leap across to the lifeboat things suddenly went wrong. At the time I was committed to jump and at a point of no return a huge wave crashed alongside, initially causing Setantii to hit the side of the lifeboat, then pushing the lifeboat and Setantii apart, leaving me hanging by my hands from the stern rails at the back of the lifeboat, and directly above the propellers. The real risk was then was that another wave would crash Setantii back against the lifeboats hull again and crushing me between them.

Second coxswain in danger over side of lifeboat with yacht menacingly close

The coxswain, Ian Fairclough, manoeuvred the lifeboat to take the stern away from the yacht but with the boots, oilskin suit and lifejacket on I was unable to swing my legs up to get back on board the lifeboat. It seemed an eternity before the lifeboat crew members realised my plight and rushed to assist and my handgrip on the rails was weakening. Luckily I was pulled aboard the lifeboat and the tow was resumed, enabling the Container Ferry that had now arrived at the river mouth, to enter Fleetwood channel without knowing of the drama that had unfolded in their path.

The Setantii crew were landed at the lifeboat station and the yacht hull, mast and rigging were brought to the shore.

The lesson for me was that when the tow parted at the top of the Fleetwood channel there were no persons on the yacht and although it would severely inconvenience the Container Ferry the risk was simply too high. I should not have gone across to re-attach the tow just to remove the obstruction. The lesson for the crew of Setantii was that they should not have attempted the crossing from the Isle of Man in such bad weather and they were lucky to get away with their lives. However, it was a job well done and three lives were saved.

Yacht Jain 29th August, 1978 - In this separate incident David Blagden was an American actor who in 1972 emigrated to England after an adventurous youth and then working as a crew member on cargo ships. He gained fame in the yachting community after taking part in a Singlehanded Transatlantic Race, in his boat Jester. He became a sailing adviser in the filming of Swallows and Amazons, and had a TV series called Plain Sailing. So a picture is portrayed of an experienced yachtsman and small boat sailor.

In his interesting book titled '*Very Willing Griffin*' he describes his transatlantic race competing against much larger ocean going yachts and gaining a creditable position against them.

In August 1978 and 34 years of age, David Blagden had been sailing his 27 foot yacht named 'Jain' in Scotland. Whilst attempting to sail his boat south to Cornwall over the Bank Holiday weekend a combination of bad weather and engine trouble forced him to call in at the Isle of Man.

His plan was then to abandon the trip to Cornwall and sail the boat to Glasson Dock near Lancaster where he would leave it for the

Book Cover - Very Willing Griffin

winter. Engine troubles persisted when they tried to leave the Isle of Man on the Sunday morning tide and they returned to harbour. By Sunday evening the weather forecast was worsening but accompanied by an experienced sailing friend Eleanora Murk-Jansen they left Ramsey Isle of Man at 10.00 p.m. on Sunday evening. Although bad weather was forecast he needed to get back to work in London as soon as possible and he did not heed the warnings of the coastguards.

The next day lifeboats from Fleetwood and Lytham were launched in gale force 8 conditions that deteriorated to Storm Force 10 following reports of distress flares off the Blackpool coast. Following an extended air sea search over a 50 square mile area, involving two lifeboats and two helicopters nothing was seen of the yacht but Eleanora's body was found on Blackpool beach the next morning. Wreckage including a mattress, bedding, compass, and a lifebelt with the name Jain on it was found along the shoreline at

Blackpool. David Blagden's body washed up on the beach at Southport one week later *(not far from where the incident with the barque Mexico had taken place in 1886). Six weeks later a fishing boat trawled up wreckage of his boat in its nets when fishing 2 miles west of Blackpool North pier.*

In this incident it was undoubtedly the need to get back for work that made an otherwise very experienced sailor take risks that he may otherwise not have taken but the consequences are life threatening.

Gynn Square Blackpool – 4th January, 1983. Sometimes in the line of duty there are incidents where fate is inexorable, or unstoppable. This happened soon after New Year in 1983 in Blackpool when a man entered into the rough seas at Blackpool seafront to save his dog and lost his life and three of 5 police officers who tried to save the man also lost their lives.

Alistair Anthony was a 25 year old Scotsman from Glasgow celebrating New Year with his parents and family at their holiday flat. He was described as being 6ft 5ins tall and a strong swimmer but he was swept off his feet by treacherous waves after trying to rescue his dog, Henry – a Jack Russell that chased a ball that bounced from the sea wall into the water. Alistair stripped off his outer clothes and was wading along the sea wall apron to try to reach Henry when he was swept into the sea. His father who was present threw a lifebelt but lost his grip on the line.

The lifeboat had been called but it was impossible to launch the Blackpool lifeboat and we were called from Fleetwood the next station up the coast, along with a rescue helicopter from RAF Valley North Wales.   Other would-be rescuers assisted and at one time had Alistair clear of the waves, suspended on a lifebelt when the rope snapped and he dropped back into the waves. Four police officers initially attended the Gynn Square location in their separate police vehicles. They had only five minutes to go before they ended their shift when they had received their call to this incident.

Police Constable Pat Abram was first to arrive and helped by others put a lifebelt around him and with a rope to the shore entered the sea – getting within 6 feet of Alistair but the line was too short to reach him, and he pulled himself back up the line to the shore. Returning to the slipway he along with PC Gordon Connolly, PC Angela Bradley, and PC Colin Morrison decided to try again. Another lifebelt rope was attached and with Colin Morrison holding the rope Pat Abram entered the water a second time. Angela Bradley had a lifeline wrapped around her waist, held by Gordon Connolly at the water's edge.

A rogue wave suddenly swept all four off their feet, so there were 5 people and a dog in the water at this time.

Emergency Service at Gynn Square   Photo: Blackpool Evening Gazette

We saw a police officer that we now know to be Pat Abram being hauled from the sea vertically up the sea wall by the lifeline tangled around his neck – the risk of strangulation or a broken neck deemed an acceptable risk. Paramedics failed to find a pulse but fought to revive him. He lived and although hospitalised for an extended period with his injuries eventually returned to work. A fifth police officer PC Martin Hewitson was also battered by the waves as he went to the bottom of the seawall slope to throw a lifebelt to the group in the water. He was later hospitalised for shock. These are the three police officers who lost their lives.

Photo: Blackpool Evening Gazette

Ian Fairclough was the lifeboat coxswain that day and I was a young 34 year old deputy coxswain of the offshore lifeboat. The weather had been bad on the way down to Blackpool, with one sea washing right over the lifeboat and the breaking waves at the scene were simply tremendous. Nothing was visible on the surface at the scene of the incident and the closest we could safety get to the sea wall was around 75 yards – about the fourth wave out from the shore. With the crew scanning the surface my recollection was of us simply holding the boat in position bow to the breaking waves as we searched slowly along the shore – and frequently shouting hang-on to the crew   as   a   breaking   sea   hit

Helicopter searching the gap between the lifeboat and the sea wall

us. For 3 hours we searched the area until the tide left insufficient water to do any more. The RAF rescue helicopter searched the gap between our-selves and the seawall – the 75 yard strip - and within half an hour the helicopter winch-man had recovered the body of 38 year old Colin Morrison. Nothing else was found on that day. Henry, the Jack Russell terrier's body was the first to be recovered from the sandbanks. Twenty three year old Angela's body was recovered from the sandbanks of Morecambe Bay by the lifeboat crew days later. Alistair Anthony's body was similarly recovered from the sandbanks on January 14th, and we didn't bring 24 year old PC Connolly's body to the shore until 27th January.

This tragedy shocked the resort, and made news around the world.

Lessons have been learned by all the services following this incident and additional equipment is carried in designated police cars in Blackpool for any incident of persons entering the water. Surprisingly, for this courageous act on behalf of the police officers who lost their lives in the icy and wind lashed sea no police decorations or awards were made, but a memorial has been erected near the spot to commemorate this incident. Perhaps the reason related to the surrounding circumstances.

Very sadly other incidents have taken place on the same promenade often when inebriated young people think they can go for a late night swim, or wave dodge in bad weather, with tragic consequences for them.

Windsurfer Rescue and R.N.L.I. Award - In the early 1980's windsurfing was a new sport enabled by the technology of modern fibre-glass available for the sailboard construction and lightweight strong materials for the mast and sail. Windsurfers were pushing the boundaries by going out in ever wilder weather conditions. In the 21st century they are a familiar sight in windy conditions, often with kites towing them along.

On Friday evening 23rd March 1984, at around 6.00 p.m., the Fleetwood lifeboat was called out to assist a windsurfer who was reported to be in trouble off the shore towards Blackpool. Near Gale force conditions existed at the lifeboat station with the wind direction from the South East, and it was well sheltered from this direction at the lifeboat station launching point. The tide was about 2½ hours after high water and at that time of year there was around one further hour of daylight. Because it would be dark within the hour and expecting some shelter from the land due to the south-easterly wind direction I decided to use the faster inshore lifeboat. At this state of tide there would still be enough water in an inshore passage called *The Neckings'* before it dried as sandbanks again within one hour. Using the inshore lifeboat would save some 45 minutes in time against getting the offshore lifeboat to the reported location of the casualty, having to go around the Wyre Channel and Lune Deeps.

The geography of the area is shown in the chart and although it was time saving there was risk in using the inflatable inshore lifeboat. The parting conversation at the lifeboat station was "Prepare to back me up with the offshore lifeboat". There was sufficient water in The Neckings but as we approached Rossall Point the sea became rougher with short breaking seas, caused by the wind over tide effect in the relatively shallow water.

Chart of Fleetwood and track through *The Neckings'* to windsurfer off Cleveleys
Source: Admiralty

Off the Western edge of the sandbanks at Rossall Point the seas were very rough with breaking waves around six to eight feet high and at the operating limits for the inshore lifeboat.

Rounding the Point we altered course to turn south towards the reported position of the casualty. With the weather deteriorating, the south-south-easterly wind had increased to gale force 8; gusting severe gale force 9, with eight to ten foot seas and a moderate to heavy swell and the inshore lifeboat was experiencing the full force of wind and sea.

Deteriorating weather and increasing seas

As we rounded the Point we realised the severe state of the sea. If you had been kneeling beside us on the deck-pad of the lifeboat looking at the cresting seas that lay in our path you would have been filled with a sense of foreboding as we were continually stung in the face by icy spray blown from the tops of the waves. In hindsight it was at this point I should have summoned assistance from the offshore lifeboat but at 25 years old I believed I could do the job and continued unaided. Throughout the passage south from the Point the lifeboat was being buffeted by rough seas. The heavy spray thrown up together with the rise and fall of the sea swell meant that visibility from the low vantage point of the inflatable boat was poor and probably not more than 50 metres. We were trying to get to the casualty position as quickly as possible but with breaking white topped seas it was necessary to slow the engine to ride these waves. We arrived at the reported position at around 18.15 hours. Close radio contact was being maintained with the Coastguard mobile officers' on the beach, who were trying to keep the sailboard under observation but as daylight was diminishing they were having difficulty in spotting the windsurfer in the increasing seas.

As inshore lifeboat lifts on one wave windsurfer spotted on another wave crest

As we were just asking for an update from the coastguard on our relative position to the windsurfer and now on the edge of darkness, the inshore lifeboat was lifted up on a high wave crest and fortuitously we caught sight of the sailboard being similarly lifted by a wave some 150 metres further out to sea, and at a distance of approximately one mile from the shore. At this moment we felt elated as we had been feeling alone and isolated amongst the breaking seas.

The survivor was sitting astride his board, which was being taken rapidly out to sea by the wind and tide. Although extremely exhausted he was still able to cling to his sailboard, and raised a hand to attract our attention in acknowledgement of seeing us as we approached him. He had already jettisoned his mast and sail. In the weather conditions there were serious risks of damaging the inflatable lifeboat if an attempt was made to take the man off the sailboard. The board sailor was wearing a dry suit and a buoyancy aid so I shouted across telling him to slip into the water and push himself clear of his board. This the man did and, as the lifeboat came alongside, he was quickly pulled on-board by the crew members.

Inshore lifeboat speeds to assist windsurfer in rough seas

For additional safety he was helped into a survivor's lifejacket on-board the inshore lifeboat. The board was then recovered, at the first attempt, and lashed to the top of the lifeboat's side sponson. The difficult decision facing us now was how to get safely back to the lifeboat station. The weather was now bad and the seas increasing and continually breaking. Two distinctly different options faced us; either head straight for the beach around 1 mile east of us and risk losing both the lifeboat and the survivor in the surf as we approached the shore, or commit to the long way back to the lifeboat station around the outside of the sandbanks of the southern shore of Morecambe Bay.

It is in the tempest of a difficult situation and when the adrenalin is flowing inside you that your inner voice as the whisper of instinct and a lifeboat coxswains friend speaks to you in helping you reason with yourself logically to choose the right pathway to recover the situation.

Because the sailor was well clad and a seemingly fit young man, I discussed our predicament with the crew and decided that trying to run the lifeboat up the beach on the nearest shore was an unnecessary risk as we could be overturned in the surf; it would be better to go back the long way, as *The Neckings* channel would be drying out by this time. The Coastguard mobile officer confirmed that, with the falling tide and rough water, *The Neckings* was no longer navigable, so we committed ourselves to the long way home.

It was now fully dark and the inflatable lifeboat was becoming sluggish at steering with an extra person on board and water in the bilge that had splashed on-board during the outward journey. The seas were too rough to drive her at full power so that she could drain off the water through her self-bailer. Essentially - the outboard engine kept going but only slow progress was made due to now following seas. At one point a large following sea picked us up and we surfed down it causing the bow to become submerged and water rolled over the forward canopy, more than half filling the lifeboat, soaking us beneath our oilskin suit to above our waists. The boat can cope with being filled with water and not sinking but there is a self-baler that should drain water out through a tube-pipe at the stern. However, you need to have some forward movement to make it effective and it was difficult to get any speed up with the large following seas to cope with. It was hard to control the heavy boat in the rough seas to stop the lifeboat being capsized but we were able to continue back towards Fleetwood.

Once round the entrance to Morecambe Bay and turning on to an east-north-easterly course, some respite was afforded by the shelter of the sandbanks. Entering the River Wyre Fleetwood main channel, and turning south-south-east for home, speed could be increased and the majority of the water was drained from the boat. A feeling of relief came over us as we knew we had made it back into the safe waters of the Fleetwood approaches and had saved the life of this windsurfer who would have undoubtedly been lost as darkness fell had we not taken the shortcut to get to his reported position.

In formal terms the records show that *'at 19.20 the inflatable lifeboat arrived back at station, where the board sailor and his board were landed. The lifeboat was re-housed and once again ready for service at 19.30'.* In personal terms the three of us collectively felt – a good job done.

Dave Owen and Stephen Musgrave

For this rescue service the service award of the RNLI was presented to me as helmsman of the D class inflatable lifeboat. Vellum service certificates were presented to crew members Barrie. E. Farmer, and David B. Owen. Subsequently, on the 26th June 1985 the RNLI Committee of Management conferred the Ralph Glister award on me and the two crew members crew members for *'the most meritorious service and bravest act of lifesaving carried out in a lifeboat under 10 metres, in the UK, in 1984'*.

As implied in these outlines of rescue 'jobs' over my twenty three years in the life-boat service I have made my own mistakes and learned lessons on every occasion. Overall I would like to feel that I have made a positive contribution and my Certificate of Service with the R.N.L.I. states that during my time over more than two decades with Fleetwood Life-boat station 215 lives were saved.

7 WILLIAM SWARBRICK RESCUES

In Chapter 1 the link was explained to my great, great, great grandfather William Swarbrick who was born in 1809; just a few years after the Battle of Trafalgar. This chapter describes three rescue incidents that William was involved with as Captain of a steam-tug.

In the 1860's William Swarbrick was Captain of the Fleetwood Harbour steam-tug 'Wyre', and harbour Pilot for ports in Morecambe Bay. Referring back to the earlier description of the developmental years of the town of Fleetwood – William Swarbrick moved there, with his family in 1846. It was the prospect of new employment that brought William Swarbrick and his young family from the family farm in the rural community of Stalmine to take advantage of the opportunity in Fleetwood.

Coastal sailing craft

This was the period before motorways and lorries; it was the early days of railways and inland waterway canals and the coastal waters around Britain were the main ways to transport goods around the country. The mid to late 1800's were a period of expansion when the sea-lanes around the shores of Great Britain were a natural and convenient highway, fundamental for moving cargo and people around the country. In the 1800's and early 1900's thousands of coastal vessels plied their trade carrying goods and raw materials to feed the needs of people and the Industrial Revolution. Vessels such as these were the white vans of their day.

Sail was still the main source of power, and international sea trade was busy importing raw materials to meet the needs of the industrial activity, including timber for construction of the new towns and their buildings. Sea going coastal vessels were plying their trade in increasing numbers, and since the 1700's lighthouses and landmarks were becoming more prevalent to improve safety of navigation. Only simple instruments were available for navigation, and in reduced visibility navigation was difficult and often relied on instinct. Weather forecasting was difficult and mariners mainly relied on weather-lore. Sea voyages were a matter of harnessing the wind, yet unable to sail directly into the wind vessels were hampered in steering their course.

The Loss of the Fleetwood Lifeboat - There is a specific purpose in mentioning this incident that happened in the third week of October 1862 when the equinoctial gales were reported in the local newspapers as being of more than the usual severity.

Steam tug *'Wyre'* of Fleetwood

Putting harbour pilots onto and taking them off vessels was the bread and butter work of the harbour tug crew, along with taking vessels in tow, and also the steam tug *'Wyre'* was frequently used to tow the lifeboat to the scene of an incident. Before lifeboats had engines it was quite normal for a harbour tug, not only in Fleetwood, to be used for towing the lifeboat out to the vicinity of a casualty. On the morning of Thursday 23rd October 1862, South West of Blackpool a schooner was seen to be in difficulties in the storm. Some portions of the vessel's sail were still set, giving rise to a belief that her crew were still alive on board. The vessel gradually drifted nearer the coast until around 2 miles from the shore where she struck the ground and soon sank, with only her masts visible above the waves.

Steam tug *Wyre* towing Fleetwood lifeboat

A telegram had been sent to Fleetwood, stating that a vessel was observed drifting about the coast off Blackpool in distress. The Fleetwood Lifeboat was immediately launched with a volunteer crew, and taken in tow by the steam-tug *Wyre*, commanded by Captain William Swarbrick. Off Blackpool the winds were of severe gale force and the sea was reported as running 'mountains high and curling over in a frightful manner', and it was decided to take the crew of the lifeboat on board the tug.

Lifeboat capsizes and tow rope parts

Subsequently the lifeboat was capsized twice by the seas but being self-righting she rolled back upright again. At one point the towline snapped and with difficulty was re-connected. Soon after that the top of the lifeboat's stern compartment was completely torn out by a heavy sea but the lifeboat was still in tow. The steam-tug *Wyre* on arriving as near as she could to the wreck found that she had sunk, with just the masts visible, and nothing living could be seen or heard, so, as the tug and lifeboat could be of no assistance they turned back.

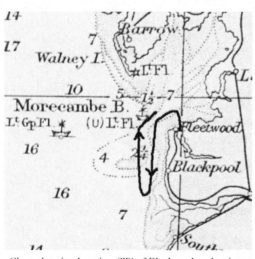

Chart showing location SW of Blackpool and point where Fleetwood Lifeboat was lost: Admiralty

The wind had meanwhile risen to a complete storm and the sea had risen considerably, and every now and then broke completely over the tug *Wyre*, causing fears for her safety and the persons on board. On the return journey the last bolt that held the lifeboat tow-rope gave way and the lifeboat drifted away into the blackness of the storm. The tug Captain turned his vessel around to attempt to recover the lifeboat, but as it was pitch dark, and the weather was so bad, the crew of the steam-tug *Wyre* quickly abandoned the search and with the lifeboat crew still on board headed back for Fleetwood, having sustained some damage to her superstructure and deck-houses.

Fleetwood lifeboat lost into the pitch darkness

Later that week the Fleetwood lifeboat was washed ashore in the north of Morecambe Bay, and arrangements were made to return the damaged hull to Fleetwood by train on a railway truck. Serious damage had been done to her port side, which had been broken open, besides other damage done to her interior. At a meeting of the Lifeboat Committee, it was resolved to make application to the National Lifeboat Institution for a ten-oared boat, which would be better than the present one.

Although he was not a member of the R.N.L.I lifeboat crew William Swarbrick played an essential role as Captain of the harbour tug *'Wyre'* that routinely took the 'rowing and sailing' lifeboat in tow, often in extreme weather conditions. In the absence of the Fleetwood lifeboat, following its loss, William and the crew of the tug *'Wyre'* undertook a number of life-saving calls in their steam tug and received awards and recognition from the government and the lifeboat service for participating in rescue incidents; in particular rescuing the Captain and crew of the barque *Pudyona*, of Glasson Dock, Lancaster in October 1862.

Steam tug 'Wyre'

The steam tug *Wyre* would have looked something like this photo from the same period, and operated from Fleetwood, regularly working as Pilot boat for vessels in Glasson Dock, Lancaster, the River Ribble for Preston, and the River Mersey for Liverpool. William Swarbrick's daughter Mrs. Eleanor Croft also recalled that the *Wyre* was one of the first vessels to take pleasure trip passengers from the North Pier, Blackpool, in the summer season, and in her early years she sailed with her father and attended to the refreshment bar along with taking tickets.

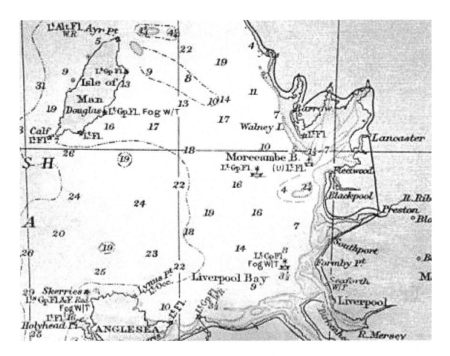

Chart of North Irish sea showing Morecambe Bay and Anglesey source: Admiralty

This chart shows the area from the North Wales Coast, Northwest England, and Morecambe Bay.

The image below is the Morecambe Bay light ship that was placed on service as a marker for the entrance to Morecambe Bay in 1863, but it wasn't there the year before when the sailing barque *Pudyona* was being towed from Holyhead (Anglesey) to Glasson Dock (Lancaster) by a steam tug named *Teazer*.

From the mid-1800's steam tugs were not only used to tow sailing vessels into and out of Port, but also to meet them in the distant approaches to a port and put a Pilot on board. This event, which led to the total loss of the *Pudyona* and the rescue of all its crew, took place just five days after the loss of the Fleetwood Lifeboat on the preceding Thursday 23rd October. So with no lifeboat available on station in Fleetwood it was the harbour tug *Wyre* with Captain Swarbrick and his crew that became involved in this rescue.

Morecambe Bay light vessel

The *Pudyona* was on a voyage from Quebec (Canada) to Glasson Dock (Lancaster) laden with a cargo of timber planks. She was in the command of Captain Foster from Lancaster. Having completed the ocean voyage sailing over 2,000 miles from Quebec, during the gales of the previous week the *Pudyona* put into Holyhead, and it was there that Captain Foster received a letter from the ship-owner Mr. Burrell in Lancaster stating that - 'following the prosperous voyage he should get a tug from Holyhead to tow *Pudyona* to Glasson Dock to ensure he was there in time to navigate up the River Lune channel on the spring tides'.

On Sunday evening 26th October 1862 *'Pudyona'* left Holyhead in tow of the Liverpool steam-tug *Teazer*, and proceeded towards Glasson Dock, a journey of around 70 miles, from the coast of Anglesey, North Wales, to Morecambe Bay. Weather forecasting was quite primitive and unreliable in the 1800's, and unexpected changes often caught out even the most experienced Captains. The weather was fine on Sunday evening, but the strong breeze that was blowing increased to gale-force from the North West before morning. Halfway through the voyage the tow-rope parted, but it was possible to re-connect to the tug *Teazer*, and continue the tow.

Barque *Pudyona* under tow from Holyhead

The two vessels proceeded towards the approaches to Morecambe Bay but not having a pilot on board they missed the deep water Lune Deep channel entrance into Morecambe Bay, and in reduced visibility on seeing Wyre Light Captain Foster realised they were too far North. Soon afterwards, in the entrance to Morecambe Bay, about 1 mile North West of Wyre Light, and less than 10 miles from her destination of Glasson Dock Lancaster the 'Pudyona' struck the stony bottom at a place called Danger Patch, breaking the tow rope connection to the tug Teazer. The force of the concussion was so great that the masts broke and the spars fell overboard, carrying all the rigging with them, and leaving the vessel at the mercy of the sea, which dashed over her in a frightful manner.

The position of the crew was truly fearful; the vessel was fast going to pieces, and with huge seas breaking over her hull, so they had difficulty saving themselves from being washed overboard. Meanwhile the *Teazer* having her tow rope, (that was trailing in the water behind the tug), to attend to decided they could not give any further assistance, abandoning the *Pudyona* and her crew to their fate. The *Pudyona* crew was just 2 miles from shore, and having sailed 2,000 miles from Canada was a mere 10 miles from their homes and families in Glasson Dock, Lancaster. Their situation was truly perilous and their vessel was beginning to break apart with the unrelenting pounding impact on the sea-bed as wave upon wave swept over their vessel.

Tug *Teazer* abandons Pudyona crew

The tug *Teazer* by this time was moving further and further away from the *Pudyona* and its crew and not returning to help. In an attempt to save themselves from being washed away the Pudyona's crew used ropes from the rigging to tie themselves to the stumps of masts in a forlorn hope of being rescued. Their feelings were of the hopelessness of their situation as the cargo of timber planks started to break away – smashing a gaping hole in the side of their ship as the force of each sea delivered further crippling blows on the wooden hull of their vessel.

Tug *Wyre* outward bound

This incident was seen by Captain Swarbrick, of the steam tug *Wyre*, as they were outward bound from Fleetwood with three pilots on board and making all speed to the assistance of another vessel that had been seen to have hoisted flag signals to indicate she was in difficulties in the bad weather.

Having seen the other incident with a dismasted vessel further off he altered course towards the tug *Teazer* and when near they shouted across to the tug *Teazer* and asked if they had got the crew of the barque on board. The *Teazer's* crew shouted back that they had not been able to rescue the crew; that is was the *Pudyona*, and the lifeboat was wanted; but the Fleetwood Lifeboat had capsized and was lost just five days earlier, and with no replacement yet available. On being told it was the *Pudyona*, Captain Swarbrick realised that it was his friend Captain Foster and his crew that the tug *Wyre* had regularly worked with in towing them from Glasson Dock on many previous voyages.

Tug *Wyre* approaches windward side of *Pudyona* hull to rescue crew

Captain Swarbrick and his crew took their steam tug *Wyre* at once to the distressed vessel, being determined to rescue those on board if possible. As the tug approached the wreck they found that the debris of the masts and rigging rendered it impossible to approach on the downwind side. Their only chance they had was to approach from the windward side, where the seas were already breaking right over the *Pudyona*, making it a very dangerous task to attempt to approach on that side as the waves would force the tug against the wrecked hull.

When the tug approached the stern of *Pudyona* to try to get alongside the wreck it could be seen that the port side was out and the cargo of timber was visible through her shattered stern. However, the minds of those on board the *Wyre* were speedily made up, and on the second attempt the tug boat was run alongside her starboard quarter, and the crew of the wrecked *Pudyona*, who had stationed themselves on that part of the vessel, leaped on board the *Wyre*, and she went off again as quickly as possible, fortunately, without having sustained any serious injury.

Rescue of *Pudyona* crew who jump onto tug *Wyre*

Almost immediately afterwards the ill-fated Pudyona was driven over the bank into the swashway, and went down in deep water.

The *Wyre*, with the crew of the *Pudyona* on board, next proceeded to the assistance of the brig *Marys*, of and for Glasson Dock, from Miramichi (Canada), with a cargo of timber. This vessel had both anchors down but they were not holding the sea-bed and the ship was dragging towards the shore and she was making signals for help and assistance.

The tug took her in tow and arrived at Glasson Dock at three o' clock in the afternoon, where she also landed the crew of the barque Pudyona, and returned to Fleetwood.

Tug *Wyre* passing Wyre Light on return to Fleetwood

The newspaper reports state - 'it is hoped that the efforts of the crew of the *Wyre* may meet with some substantial reward at the hands of the Board of Trade for their conduct on this occasion'.

Crowds greeted tug *Wyre* with her survivors

Silver Medal of the Royal National Lifeboat Institution - In recognition of the services rendered in rescuing the seventeen crew of the barque *Pudyona* Captain William Swarbrick and Pilot Robert Gerard were each awarded the silver medal of the Royal National Lifeboat Institution at a meeting of the R.N.L.I. on Thursday 1st January 1863, in Liverpool.

Presentation of a Telescope to Captain William Swarbrick.

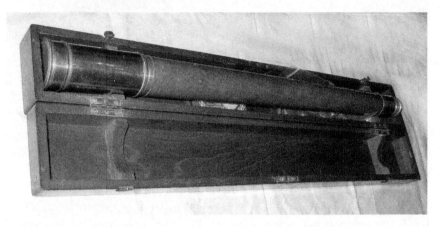

Inscribed telescope presented to William Swarbrick

A report from Fleetwood Chronicle, Blackpool Herald & Lytham Gazette 19th December, 1862 states:

'Yesterday, a telescope was presented to Captain Swarbrick, of the steam-tug *Wyre*, having been sent as a recognition of his courageous and humane conduct, by her Majesty's government, in rescuing from imminent peril of shipwreck the crew of the barque *Pudyona*, stranded in Morecambe bay, on the 27th October. We gave the particulars at the time, and we have now the pleasure to record that the gallant services of Captain Swarbrick and his crew, have not passed unrewarded. The presentation took place in the Estate Office, Fleetwood, J.S. Burrell, Esq., of Lancaster in the chair, to which he was voted by the unanimous voice of the meeting. The room was filled with gentlemen of the town, most of them interested in shipping'.

The telescope, in its wooden case, that was presented to William Swarbrick is now in the possession of a descendent Claire Swarbrick who lives in Leicestershire.

The following letter from the owner of the barque Pudyona is held in Fleetwood Museum.

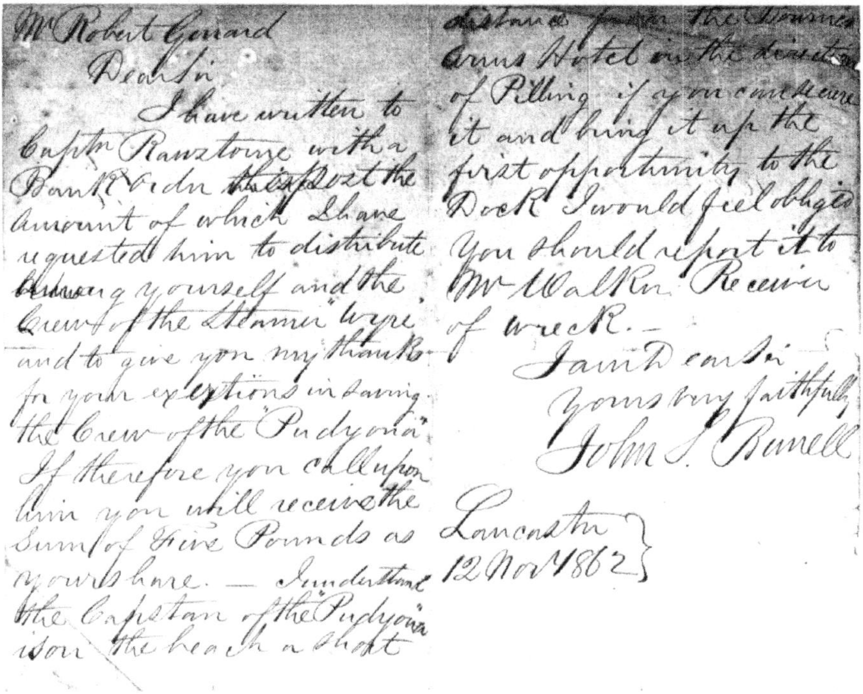

Mr Robert Gerrard
Dear Sir
I have written to Captn Rawstorne with a Bank Order the post the amount of which I have requested him to distribute among yourself and the Crew of the Steamer "Wyre" and to give you my thanks for your exertions in saving the Crew of the "Pudyona" If therefore you call upon him you will receive the sum of Five Pounds as your share. — I understand the Capstan of the Pudyona is on the beach a short distance from the Bourne Arms Hotel in the direction of Pilling if you can secure it and bring it up the first opportunity to the Dock I would feel obliged You should report it to Mr Walker Receiver of Wreck. —
I am Dear Sir
Yours very faithfully
John S. Burrell
Lancaster
12 Nov 1862

It reads:

Mr. Robert Gerrard,

I have written to Captain Rawstrone with a Bank Order in the post the amount of which I have requested him to distribute among yourself and the Crew of the Steamer *'Wyre'* and to give you my thanks for your exertions in saving the Crew of the *'Pudyona'*.

If therefore you call upon him you will receive the sum of Five Pounds as your share. I understand the Capstan of the *'Pudyona'* is on the beach a short distance from the Bourne Arms Hotel in the direction of Pilling if you could secure it and bring it up the first opportunity to the Dock I would feel obliged.

You should report it to Mr. Walker Receiver of Wreck.

I am Dear Sir

Yours very faithfully,

John S. Burrell

Lancaster
12 Nov 1862

Another incident involving William Swarbrick and the tug *Wyre* occurred almost twenty years to the day before the R.N.L.I.'s most serious catastrophe when the barque Mexico of Hamburg was wrecked and the crews of St. Annes and Southport lifeboats were lost whilst attempting to save the lives of the crew of Mexico near Ainsdale, Southport Lancashire.

Barque *'Inga'* of Norway - This incident was some four years later than the *Pudyona* rescue, when on 7th December, 1866, distress signals were seen West of Fleetwood in Lancashire. The *'Wyre'* steam-tug, with Captain Swarbrick, took the Fleetwood life-boat *'Child of Hale'* along with her crew in tow through an inshore channel called The Neckings off Fleetwood promenade, and after some time, discovered the vessel two miles further out than had been expected.

Fleetwood lifeboat *Child of Hale* approaching barque *Inga* of Kragona Norway

The lifeboat was towed to windward of the wreck, and then cast off by the tug, the lifeboat crew using their oars to get alongside the vessel. It proved to be the *Inga*, a Norwegian barque of Kragona a port in Norway near Oslo, with Captain Larsen, and a crew of 12 men all told. The barque *Inga* was on passage from Miramichi (a timber port in New Brunswick, near Quebec, Canada), with a cargo of timber, for Fleetwood. She was rolling fearfully in the troughs of the rough sea with two anchors down, one with 75 fathoms

120

chain and the other with 45 fathoms chain, in 22 fathoms of water. Captain Larsen had taken a Liverpool pilot on board off Point Lynas two days previously and was proceeding safely on his course when caught by the gale on Thursday night. Having 22 fathoms of water beneath them the pilot dropped both anchors hoping that the vessel might hold until the weather moderated. Around three o' clock on Friday morning it was realised that she was not holding her ground and was drifting towards the shore. The pilot therefore ordered the masts to be cut away. This was done with just the fore mast remaining as the main and mizzen masts had been cut away as the lifeboat was arriving.

Projecting yard and debris as masts were cut away

Subsequently they cut away the remaining for'ard mast. Unfortunately, at the moment when it fell, the vessel plunged to leeward, which laid the mast on the deck, with one yard projecting over the vessel's side from twelve to twenty feet. When the lifeboat *Child of Hale* arrived alongside there was not room on the lee side to take off the crew either fore or aft of the wooden yard arm that hung menacingly as a dangerous obstacle over the lee side of the *Inga*. Every roll of the vessel threatened to plunge the yard down onto the lifeboat to annihilate her and her brave crew as she approached the stranded vessel.

The crew of the lifeboat, however, pulled towards the protruding yard, and securing a rope forward, with great difficulty they commenced the rescue of the ship's crew. Several dropped into the boat from the projecting yard, when an enormous wave lifted the life-boat upwards against the yard, pressing the lifeboat far down into the water. This occurred four times before the life-boat got clear of the wreck. On one of these occasions four oars were broken, along with all the rowlocks on the lee side, and the life-boat's hull was also partially stove in and damaged.

The Steamer *"Wyre,"* of Fleetwood, Captain Wm. Swarbrick, towing the Lifeboat of the Royal National Lifeboat Institution to the dismasted Barque *"Inga,"* of Norway, December 7th 1866, on

The remainder of the crew of the *Inga* dropped into the lifeboat forward of the yard, the last man to leave being the cook, who brought with him the captain's portmanteau. As no one was left on board the *Inga* to cast off the rope by which the lifeboat was secured. It had to be cut and as the crew was prevented using their oars by the destruction of oars and rowlocks, the lug-sail, the only sail usable on board the lifeboat was hoisted and in two hours the crew of the unfortunate vessel were landed at Fleetwood. The lifeboat had twenty-six persons on-board on her return voyage but the coxswain brought the survivors and his crew safely back to Fleetwood.

It was for the rescue of the thirteen persons from the *Inga* that the grateful Norwegian ship-owners on hearing of the circumstances of this rescue commissioned a pastel drawing that captures with Victorian drama the steam-tug *Wyre* towing the lifeboat to the incident.

For 110 years this picture hung in the former Fleetwood Lifeboat house until the wooden structure was de-commissioned in 1976, when it was transferred to Lancashire Records Office. It now hangs in the current Fleetwood Lifeboat house near the Ferry.

William Swarbrick holding telescope

Captain William Swarbrick was my great, great, great grandfather and a family photograph shows him holding the telescope that was presented to him for his role in the rescue of the captain and crew of the barque 'Pudyona' of Glasson Dock, Lancaster.

William Swarbrick died on 5th July 1889, at the age of 79 years. He was described in the Fleetwood Chronicle as 'an old and well respected inhabitant of Fleetwood, and a gentleman who for many years occupied a prominent position in maritime circles'. The report of his death states that he came to Fleetwood 43 years ago, when he worked as a pilot on the boats which ran between Liverpool and Fleetwood. In the year 1855 he was appointed under the North Lancashire Steam Navigation Co., as a master of the tug-boats on the River Wyre, in which capacity he served till ten years ago, when he retired through failing health. The report continues that the deceased was interred at the Fleetwood Cemetery on Monday last. Deceased leaves a family of two sons and three daughters. Mr. E. Swarbrick, painter, &c., is his son.

(Fleetwood Chronicle Reportage, Friday 11th July, 1889).

William Swarbrick's Pilot Licence is preserved in the archives of Lancashire Records Office, along with other artefacts.

In her book 'Shipwrecks in the North-West' Catherine Rothwell (1983), an author local to Fleetwood records that *'Such a salt of the sea was Captain William Swarbrick .... hands like cabbage leaves he could fell a man at one blow but was as gentle as a lamb with his wife'*. In correspondence with Catherine in 2007 she informed me that a relation came to Fleetwood Library with a number of artefacts, including William Swarbricks pilots licence that are now held at Lancashire Records Office, Preston, and it was in conversation with the relative that this remark was passed on.

Stephen Musgrave

8 THE GREAT GALES/THE LATE GALES

In Victorian times the newspapers of that day often used generic headlines of 'The Great Gales/The Late Gales' as umbrella titles beneath which individual incidents of wrecks and rescues were featured. This chapter includes an eclectic mix of life-saving incidents to broaden the scope and perspective of this book, and illuminate the wider role of the lifeboat service.

Fishing Smack *Osprey* and Schooner *Jean Campbell* - The incident of the Fleetwood fishing smack '*Osprey*' and a schooner '*Jean Campbell*', led to the loss of three lives that are commemorated by a memorial in the Euston Park, Fleetwood.

On the 7th of November, 1890 an exceptionally violent storm was experienced on the Lancashire coast. At the height of this storm distress signals were spotted in the direction of Bernard Wharf, and the Fleetwood Lifeboat '*Child of Hale*' lifeboat was launched at 6.00 a.m. in the morning, being towed out by the steam-tug *Wardleys*. On reaching the casualty, Coxswain Robert Wright dropped anchor and the lifeboat was slowly manoeuvred towards the vessel, which was found to be the barque' *Labora*' of Egersund near Stavanger on the Southwest coast of Norway, but due to the violent seas it was too difficult to get alongside. The crew of the *Labora* then passed a lifebuoy with a rope attached and floated this towards the lifeboat and the crew picked this up. The line was secured and the breeches-buoy rigged, by means of which, one by one, the whole crew of 13 men were dragged through the icy waves and hauled aboard the lifeboat, the rescue taking 2 hours to complete, and the lifeboat then returned to Fleetwood with the survivors.

Shortly after they had been landed news was received that another vessel was in distress and so the lifeboat-men quickly manned the No.2 lifeboat '*Edith*' and they slipped the moorings at 3.00 p.m., the life-boat then being taken in tow by the steam-tug *Wardleys* again. This casualty was found to be the 495 ton barque '*New Brunswick*', with a crew of 11 persons. She had lost all her masts and these, together with all the rigging, were trailing over the side making it extremely difficult for the lifeboat to approach. But, with great skill and in spite of the huge seas that were sweeping clean over the vessel, Coxswain Wright took the lifeboat close enough to rescue the whole crew.

The *Osprey's* boat sinks on the return journey

Also during this violent storm, while the local fishing smack *'Osprey'*, under the command of James Fogg, was struggling to reach Fleetwood safely, the crew of the *'Osprey'* sighted the schooner *'Jean Campbell'*, which was in distress, with her crew signalling for assistance. James Fogg took the *'Osprey'* in as close as he could and then, under his guidance, a small boat was launched, manned by George Wilkinson, James Abram, and George Greenall. After a desperate struggle in the violent seas, they succeeded in rescuing the schooner's crew of three men. But, tragically, as the small boat headed back towards the *'Osprey'*, it was swamped and sank. The three crew of the *'Jean Campbell'* were drowned along with James Abram and George Greenall; the only survivor being George Wilkinson, who was hauled to safety by James Fogg and the smack's cook. For their courageous efforts to save the crew of the *'Jean Campbell'*, James Fogg and George Wilkinson were each awarded a Silver Medal by the R.N.L.I.

In these rescue incidents it is the people and their stories that are the poignant elements of these narratives and in much the same way as the sinking of the Titanic is remembered in part for the trio led by Wallace Hartley playing 'Nearer my God to Thee', in newspaper accounts following the *Osprey* and *Jean Campbell* incident the hymn 'Pull for the Shore' was a poignant reminder of the lost colleagues of the fishermen and their families. The Fleetwood Chronicle reported that on the following Sunday evening a memorial service was held by the Fleetwood Corp of the Salvation Army in the Albert Hall Fleetwood to the memory of James Abram, one of the fishermen who lost their lives whilst heroically endeavoring to rescue the crew of the schooner Jean Campbell, and who was also a member of the Salvation Army. A number of fishermen sang together the hymn Pull for the Shore, which was the last which Abram was heard to sing at their gathering on the Monday previous to the sad disaster. George Clarkson, a fisherman, and also a member of the corps, spoke a few words, referring to the last occasion on which Abram was amongst them and pleading with the young men present to follow in the footsteps of their dear departed friend, and give themselves to God. Another soldier, named Thomas Sharpe, stepped forward to speak a few words, but he was too moved to say much. He alluded to Abram as having been a good "backstay" to him in the hour of temptation. In speaking of their deceased brother, he said they had had many walks together, and he little thought on returning home that he would never again see him on earth. They had all heard of the heroic deed when Abram and his companions launched their small boat to save the lives of others, though it meant to them death and a watery grave. They were young men cut off in their youth, and he wanted to know how those present would fare if it were their turn next? In conclusion, he urgently appealed to them to turn to the God in whom Abram had found peace.

George Wilkinson, who was saved, stated that when the crew of the schooner Jean Campbell was taken off their vessel into the small boat they thought they were in perfect safety. The captain of the sinking schooner turned round and said it was time they were off the accursed thing, at the same time making use of an oath. Even in such peril, and at such a moment, Abram had remembered his God, and checked the man. As he did so the fatal wave came and overturned the boat, and five of the six people on board perished.

A fund was set-up locally for the dependents of James Abram and George Greenall to commemorate this incident and a Monument to their gallantry was erected in the ornamental gardens in the Euston Park.

Monument in Euston Park Fleetwood

Princess Victoria Disaster - A 'Great Gale' on the last day of January 1953 is remembered for a number of reasons, foremost of which is the loss of (British Rail/Ship) BR/S *Princess Victoria* and 132 of its 172 passengers and crew. It is also remembered for 'The Great Storm' when winds reaching over 100 miles per hour swept from the Atlantic Ocean across the British Isles. The winds whipped up the abnormally high tide, which battered the coastal defences in Scotland and Northern Ireland and caused flooding along the North Sea coast of East Anglia. No fewer than 300 people lost their lives at sea during the storm. However the greatest single tragedy was that of the Larne-Stranraer ferry, the *Princess Victoria*.

The Princess Victoria was launched in 1947 and was designed to carry passengers, vehicles and cargo. The after end and her stern were open, except for a five and a half foot high steel door. It was more like a gate and folded back in two parts to allow cars to be loaded and unloaded. Captain Ferguson, a well-experienced seaman who lived in Stranraer, headed the ship's crew, who mainly lived in either Stranraer or Larne. Most had worked on the 'railway ships' for many years. The ship's profile was not dissimilar to the Isle of Man Steamers that ran from Fleetwood to Douglas in the 1950's and 60's.

According to survivors, it never occurred to anyone on board that the sailing on the morning of the 31st January from Stranraer would be different to any other. It was clearly going to be an uncomfortable crossing as high winds prevented the crane loading some of the cargo on board, delaying the ships departure from berth. However, at 8.00 a.m. that morning, the ship was making its way from Stranraer towards the mouth of Loch Ryan. Its passengers included the North Down MP Sir Walter Smiles and the then Deputy Prime Minister Major Maynard Sinclair. Some observers say that the presence of the two politicians is the only reason the ship sailed in such bad weather on that day. The ship discovered the first 'big sea' soon after passing Cairn Ryan. According to witnesses from the time, the ship met 'a howling gale and a horrific rolling sea' that attacked the ship from all sides as it travelled towards open sea at the mouth of Loch Ryan. To try to control the ship, Captain Ferguson sailed northwards. The inquiry into the disaster was told by survivors that at some point soon after reaching the open waters of the Irish Sea the decision was made to turn back towards Stranraer. Circumstances took over having turned the ship around, when a huge wave forced open the steel doors at the stern on the car deck, buckling them in the process. Crew members sent to inspect the damage were met by a torrent of water inside the car deck. Soon afterwards a Morse code communication began from the Princess Victoria to Portpatrick Wireless Station. In turn the Wireless Station radioed the coastguard with the message *"Princess Victoria to Portpatrick Wireless Station - Hove to off mouth of Loch Ryan. Vessel not under command. Urgent assistance of Tug required."* It is, in hindsight, somewhat ironic that two ocean going tugs had been in Lough Ryan only 2 days before. The two tugs in question had set sail for Douglas, Isle of Man arriving in their home port earlier that day. Portpatrick lifeboats was launched and began communication with Portpatrick Radio. Aircraft from RAF Aldergrove; a naval frigate HMS Contest; the oil tanker Pass of Drumocter; the cargo ship Lairdsmoor and a trawler, the Eastcoates were also involved in the search for Princess Victoria.

British Rail Ship *Princess Victoria*

In normal conditions, the area would have been busy with cross-channel traffic, but many were not sailing that day, instead taking shelter in Belfast Lough. One of the first problems was that the fact that the Princess Victoria was only able to communicate in Morse Code, while all the other ships and stations were only able to communicate by radiotelephony. This led to delays in communicating important information between all the parties concerned over the next few hours. It also hampered attempts to ascertain the Princess Victoria's true location. The ship's crew estimated, in the terrible conditions, that the ship was close to the Scottish Coast. It was to that area, therefore, that the rescue ships headed, 10 miles away from the Victoria's actual position.

It was not until 13.35, when the ship was in real danger that the message came through that the Victoria's crew had spotted the coast of Northern

Ireland and could see the Mew Island lighthouse on the Copeland Islands. Suddenly, the ships sheltering in Belfast Lough realised how close the stricken vessel was to their location. On board the ship, initially, passengers were kept calm by frequent reassuring messages from the Bridge. The crew, it would seem, did not foresee sinking as an option. Around midday, the captain had announced the ship was passing through a period of grave emergency and those life jackets would be distributed. The ship was already listing to 45 degrees at this point. Passengers were gathered, mainly, in the lounge and smoking rooms at the top of the hip. As the ship listed further, the situation aboard became more critical. Passengers had difficulty moving around, as the walls had, in effect, become the floor. Many tried to make their way to the life rafts via the highest point on the ship. The male passengers and crew assisted women and children.

When the life rafts launched, some were overcome by waves and broke up in the water, leaving their occupants in the sea. At 13.30, the order was given to abandon ship, but by then, passengers had begun to be washed into the sea. At the same time, the Donaghadee Lifeboat, the Sir Samuel Kelly, was launched. The Lifeboat men were fully aware of the conditions at sea. The Lifeboat was beginning a period of 24 hours at sea. At 13.58, David Broadfoot, the Victoria's radio operator sent what would be his last message; "SOS estimated position now 5 miles east of Copelands, Entrance Belfast Lough". Then the communications ceased. According to survivors, the Victoria rolled over and slid under the waves just after 2pm. Ernie Jardine was the radio operator at Portpatrick Radio station, and he was the only person to pick up the SOS call from the Princess Victoria and he kept communications open with David Broadfoot throughout the distress period. The ship's radio officer, David Broadfoot, was posthumously awarded the George Cross for staying at his post to the very end, allowing passengers and crew to escape, even though by doing so he was preventing his own escape. His medal is on permanent display in Stranraer Museum. In later life Ernie as a Radio Surveyor regularly conducted examinations in radio qualifications for students at Fleetwood Nautical College. In 2003 he appeared on the BBC TV Timewatch documentary 'The Greatest Storm' recalling this disaster. Ernie passed away in January, 2015.

The first rescue ship on the scene was the 'Orchy' and arrived around 14.40. Its crew reported seeing survivors in the water and on rafts. An aircraft also arrived to assist and reported the same scenario. The 'Pass of Drumocter' was the next ship to arrive in the area and attempted to rescue the survivors. The Donaghadee lifeboat arrived at the same time and assisted the other ships in rescuing 33 people. Portpatrick lifeboat also assisted in the rescue efforts. Both lifeboats made for Donaghadee where the Imperial Hotel had become the headquarters of the emergency operation. With all the survivors accounted for, the grim search for bodies began, again involving a number of ships and lifeboats. Due to the high seas and strong currents, bodies were found in various areas from the Scottish Coast to the Isle of Man.

The sinking of the Princess Victoria on 31st January 1953 with the loss of 135 lives, was one of the worst maritime disasters in the waters of the British Isles. The Donaghadee lifeboat, Sir Samuel Kelly, rescued 34 from the disaster with its coxswain Hugh Nelson being awarded a Bronze Medal and the British Empire Medal for the skill, courage and initiative shown during the rescue. In the days after, the tragic event was marked by remembrance services in Donaghadee, Larne and Stranraer. The *Sir Samuel Kelly* lifeboat has been preserved in Donaghadee and fund raising events were organised to find a permanent shelter to home this historic heritage lifeboat.

Many questions have been asked since the tragedy. One concerns the unheeded warnings, caused by incidents on the ship in the preceding years. On 25th October 1949, the ship was carrying milk tankers when some broke free from their holding lines in rough sea. The ship started to list and made its way slowly to Stranraer. Due to the list, it could not dock and some of the tankers had to be emptied. The delay in the wasted milk getting into the sea showed the scuppers, there to carry seawater off the car decks were too small to cope with a large amount of liquid. In November 1951, the ship met a heavy sea in Larne harbour. The seawater entered the car deck and again the small scuppers could not discharge the water quickly. This led to another dangerous journey across the Irish Sea. These issues should have shown a major problem that if fixed at the time, may have prevented the tragedy.

The official inquiry into the tragedy was held at Crumlin Road Courthouse in Belfast in March 1953. It lasted for 25 days and resulted in a 30,000-word document. Two main reasons were given for the loss; the inadequacy of the stern doors, which yielded under pressure from the sea and the inadequacy of the clearing arrangements for the water, which accumulated on the deck, causing the starboard list culminating in the ship capsizing and sinking. The *Eastcoates* was in command of Skipper David Brewster, of Fleetwood, who, I believe, received the British Empire Medal for his efforts. He had been brought up with his siblings by Dr Barnado's Homes; the quietly-spoken, pipe-smoking Dave was every inch the under-stated hero. At the inquiry Skipper Brewster was asked to describe the motion of his vessel in the weather at the time. "In bad weather", he said "a trawler will do anything but turn over".

The tragedy is one, which has touched many in the British Isles. The fact it occurred within living memory and that some of the survivors and rescuers are still alive make this major incident all the more poignant. It is of some consolation that the terrible events of the 31st January 1953 paved the way for major changes in the structure of future ro-ro ferries and lessons were learnt that may have saved lives since. Lessons were learned from this incident. In the RNLI in the same way that the Rohilla incident at Whitby pushed forward the transition to motor lifeboats, so with communications the Princess Victoria incident led to a review and improvement of telecommunications at sea. However, the major lesson learned from this tragic incident has revolutionised that way that Ro-Ro ferries are designed with watertight doors on the vehicle deck.

Steam Trawler Michael Griffiths - It was during this same storm that the 286 ton Fleetwood Steam Trawler *Michael Griffiths* was lost with her 13 crew off the west coast of Scotland, some 7 to 8 miles South of Barra Head at the bottom end of Islay on 31st January, 1953. She was a home waters trawler owned by the Clifton Steam Trawler Limited Company, fishing the grounds of the West Coast of Scotland. She had sailed earlier on Thursday 29th January with the families of the crew waving goodbye from the Ferry Beach, but she returned to the port of Fleetwood for repairs to an oil feed pump valve. Following this repair she departed in the early hours of Friday 30th January, at around 12.30 a.m. By Friday evening she had reached the Inner Hebrides and around 8.30 p.m. was sighted 'dodging' the seas in the deteriorating weather South-West of Dubh Artacht Light. She was last seen at around 23.10 p.m. that night by another Fleetwood trawler *Aigret* (FD180) and by this time the weather was reported to be North-West sever gale force 9, veering between North-North-West (NNW) and increasing to force 10, with snow, and very rough seas and 30 foot waves.

S.T. Michael Griffith. Lost with all hands in the Great Gale of 1953

Around 09.23 a.m. on the following morning (31st January, 1953) two other Fleetwood trawlers, the '*Velia*' (FD116) and '*Wyre General*' (FD258) heard a radio-telephone distress message from the '*Michael Griffiths*'. This stark message stated that she was 7-8 mile south of Barra Head, 'full of water – no steam – helpless', and asking 'will some ship please come and help us'. The *Velia* and *Wyre General* were too far away to be of direct assistance, but they assisted in relaying the distress message. Two other trawlers 'Wardour' (GY253) and Braconbank (A237) proceeded towards the reported position, even though they were at least 85 miles away, and the weather conditions were appalling. Castlebay and Islay lifeboats launched to assist and searched the area south of Barra Head for seven hours, but didn't find anything.

A naval vessel was ordered to sail from Londonderry, and reported the weather conditions in the search area to be 100 m.p.h. winds, with waves of 50 feet, and a snow storm. An air sea search was also carried out by the R.A.F., but the air and sea searches were in vain.

The town of Fleetwood was in shock as word reached the port that this trawler was missing. The families of the thirteen crew waited in hope, but it was a few days later when two lifebuoys bearing the trawler marking of the *Michael Griffiths* were found near Loch Foyle, Northern Ireland, dashing hopes that the vessel would be found. Further wreckage was found a week later on 7th February when the ship's lifeboat from the *Michael Griffiths* was washed ashore on Inishtrahull County Donegal. Nothing was found of the 13 crew who perished in the *Michael Griffiths* in this great gale.

The three day formal inquiry conducted by the Government's Ministry of Transport in Fleetwood in April of that year (1954) was unable to establish the cause of this disaster, but concluded that the trawlers loss was due to 'exceptionally heavy weather'. The inquiry was satisfied that the vessel was seaworthy, properly equipped and her radio apparatus was in a satisfactory condition.

A corollary to this sad incident was that two of the crew members of the Portaskaig, Islay, lifeboat also lost their lives during the search for the *Michael Griffiths*. They were second coxswain Alexander MacNeil (24 yrs) who was the younger brother of the coxswain Duncan MacNeil, and crewman John MacTaggart (39 yrs). The life-boat had been called out twice that night and during the search for the trawler *Michael Griffiths* there was a severe gale blowing with waves washing right over the lifeboat into the cockpit. The lifeboat coxswain said it was "a very wild night and the worst wind at sea in his long experience". The lifeboat mechanic saw MacTaggart going in and out of the engine room, because sometimes crew members would go there for warmth. At 05.00 a.m. the mechanic entered the engine room and saw both men in a sitting position, appearing to be asleep. He reported this to the coxswain who thought they were probably sea-sick, but went to investigate and found both men unconscious. They were pulled out into the cockpit where artificial respiration was commenced but they did not respond. Although the men had died from carbon monoxide poisoning no defect was found in the engine exhaust system. The accident was blamed on the extreme weather with huge seas breaking over the life-boat exhaust funnel, blowing back fumes into the engine room.

The lifeboat service continues to rely on volunteers. Naturally, many improvements have been made to lifeboat design and construction, yet the single most important factor is the crew members, for without their skills and bravery the best materials would be useless.

9 The Past and The Future

R.N.L.B. Ann Letitia Russell - was operational as Fleetwood Lifeboat from 1939 until 1976. Built at Cowes on the Isle of Wight at the boat yard of Groves and Guttridge she was a 41 foot 'Watson' class but it was not a self-righting hull.

Re-housing the Ann Letitia Fleetwood Lifeboat

She was originally powered by two 35 horse power 'Weyburn' petrol engines, giving a service speed of just over 8 knots. These engines were replaced by twin Parsons Porbeagle 47 horse power diesel engines in 1963, improving the operational reliability. Both propellers were located in 'shaft tunnels' to offer some protection above the keel, so that the lifeboat could be taken into shallow water without damaging the propellers. The engine controls were beside the steering position towards the stern of the boat. A chart recording depth sounder was also mounted in view of the steering wheel to show the depth of water beneath the keel and the contour of the sea-bed. Communication equipment in the 1960's comprised a Medium Frequency (MF) radio-telephony trans-ceiver, a marine Very High Frequency (VHF) short range radio-telephone and a Ultra High Frequency (UHF) radio-telephone for communication with a rescue helicopter.

The cost of building this lifeboat was £6,634 and this was provided from a legacy donation to the R.N.L.I by the late Miss Ann Russell, and at a service of naming and dedication she was christened Ann Letitia Russell after the benefactor's mother. Ann had earlier bequeathed money that was used to fund the new Montrose Lifeboat named John Russell in memory of her father.

There was little protection from the elements for the crew. The coxswain stood in the open at the steering position and the crew members generally stood on the exposed side decks. A wooden spray dodger was the only cover for the engine controls, instruments and engine-room access hatch. A smaller wooden canopy was towards the bow and used for a rope store. Although it was normal to get wet on a service call the Ann Letitia' was a fantastic 'go anywhere' sea boat, giving ordinary men a tool with which they could undertake extraordinary tasks and get life-saving results, even in the wildest weather.

Following thirty seven years of active service at Fleetwood she was retired into the Reserve Fleet of the R.N.L.I., where she was bought and used for a short time as a Pilot boat in a harbour in Ireland. More recently she was converted into a pleasure craft on the East Anglian coast but around 2009 she had been brought ashore from the Marina at Lowestoft. She then languished on the harbour wall until the owner contacted the Fleetwood Weekly News who published a news report and a group was formed to bring this former lifeboat back to its home port.

Sufficient funds were raised by well-wishers during Summer 2015 to pay for transportation back to Fleetwood and work commenced to strip off non-original fittings in preparation for a restoration project to locate and display her as an attraction for visitors on Fleetwood Promenade, by her 80th birthday in 2018.

R.N.L.B. Kenneth James Pierpoint - The Tyne Class offshore lifeboat William Street will have been on station at Fleetwood for over 25 years when replaced in Spring 2016 by the new Shannon Class offshore lifeboat named RNLB Kenneth James Pierpoint, and with a service speed of 25 knots.

Shannon Class R.N.L.B Kenneth James Pierpoint

Kenneth Pierpoint was a R.A.F. pilot during the Second World War and passed away tragically on 28th August 1942, at the age of 20. His sister Kathleen Mary Pierpoint, from Altrincham, Cheshire, left the majority of her estate to the RNLI charity, in memory of her brother, when she died on 31st May, 2012. To commemorate this generosity the new Shannon lifeboat will bear his name following the dedication ceremony at the Fleetwood lifeboat station.

The Shannon is the latest class of all-weather lifeboat to join the lifeboat fleet and the first to be propelled by waterjets instead of traditional propellers, making it the most agile and manoeuvrable all-weather lifeboat yet. It is designed to be launched and recovered from a beach as well as lie afloat.

Designed entirely in-house by a team of RNLI engineers, the RNLI has harnessed cutting-edge technology to ensure this new lifeboat meets the demands of a 21st century rescue service, building on systems developed for its big sister, the Tamar class. The Shannon will gradually replace the Mersey and Tyne class lifeboats, which are now nearing the end of their operational lives. Once the Shannon Class lifeboats are placed on station, the entire all-weather lifeboat fleet will be capable of 25 knots, making the lifeboat service more efficient and effective than ever before.

The Shannon is designed to be inherently self-righting, returning to an upright position in the event of capsize. Its unique hull is designed to minimise slamming of the boat in heavy seas. And shock-absorbing seats further protect the crew from impact when powering through the waves. A Systems and Information Management System (SIMS) allows the crew to operate and monitor many of the lifeboat's functions from the safety of five of   the   six   seats.

The naming of the Shannon class lifeboats follows a tradition of naming lifeboats after rivers. However, it is the first time an Irish river has been chosen. The River Shannon is 240 miles in length and is the longest river in Ireland. Although each Shannon class lifeboat is expected to have an operational lifetime of 25 years, the life expectancy of the Shannon's hull and wheelhouse is 50 years. So after 25 years of service, each Shannon lifeboat will undergo a total refit where the machinery, systems and equipment will be renewed or replaced and the hull and wheelhouse reused – creating a new Shannon class lifeboat ready to save lives at sea for a further 25 years.

10 BIBLIOGRAPHY

Blagden. D. (1973) Very Willing Griffen Peter Davies.

Farr, A.D., (1973). Let not the Deep. Impulse Publications

Lennox Kerr, A., (1954). The Great Storm. Harrap

Sefton Libraries(2001). The Great Lifeboat Disaster of 1886. Sefton Council.

Kilroy. F., (1998) The Wreck of the Mexico. Lytham R.N.L.I.

Hennessy. S. (2010). Women of the RNLI History Press.

Rothwell. C. (2009). Shipwrecks of the North-West Coast. History Press.

Mattson.A.S., (2009). The Tragic Wreck of the Bristol and The Mexico on the South Shore of Long Island. (Amazon.com)

Admiralty Charts. Burrow Head to Liverpool chart

11 ACKNOWLEDGEMENTS

Thanks go to the Blackpool Evening Gazette for assistance with archive research of lifeboat incidents, use of photographs and access to reportage of 19th century events.

Thanks also to the following for permission to use pictures and images:

Lancashire County Council Museum Service and Fleetwood Museum for use of the image of the tug Wardleys towing Fleetwood Lifeboat Maude Pickup to a rescue.

Sefton Libraries Information Services for images of the Southport and St. Annes lifeboat crew.

Lytham Lifeboat Museum for images of the St. Annes lifeboat.

Kirkleatham Museum, Redcar and Cleveland Museum Service. The Launch of the Runswick Bay Lifeboat by the Women of Runswick. Artist T. Brown.

The Laing Gallery, Newcastle The Women by Artist John Charlton.

Lowry Collection, Salford. A Volunteer for the Lifeboat.

Fleetwood Lifeboat station for use of lifeboat images

Thanks also to David Pearce and John Swannie for their Forewords and proof-reading the book draft.

Particular appreciation to local artist Ron Baxter for his illustrations throughout this book.

Thanks to Derek Eaton at Lighthouse Stationers Fleetwood for his patience in copying the diagrams and early drafts of this book.

ABOUT THE AUTHOR

Dr Stephen Musgrave was born in Burnley, raised in Fleetwood Lancashire and now lives in Stalmine.

Having trained for a career at sea as a Merchant Navy Radio Officer he came ashore and taught in a mono-technic Nautical establishment that merged to become part of a Further Education College. Before semi-retiring he worked in Higher Education with the Open University managing a professional development programme for staff in the Schools' sector in Information & Communication Technology.

He holds a Ph.D. in Telematics – the science of Computing and Electronic Telecommunications, with a specialist interest in Portal systems.

For twenty three years he was involved in the lifeboat service in Fleetwood, serving as Deputy Coxswain for 12 years. He received the Royal National Lifeboat Institution service award for the most meritorious rescue in the UK in 1984, in a Lifeboat under 10 metres, when a windsurfer got into difficulties in gale force conditions in Morecambe Bay.

This book gives a perspective of his time as a crew member and officer in the lifeboat service, and an account of his ancestor's link with the lifeboat service in the nineteenth century. The focus is on 'people' aspects of the R.N.L.I. and the changes from the 19th to the 21st century.

Printed in Great Britain
by Amazon

22971786R00086